TATTOOS:

The Ultimate Proof of a Successful Brand

Denise Wymore

Jacket photo and book design by Gina Nass

Photo taken at Electric Dragonland Tattoo Studio, Hopkins, MN

(952) 933-2097 · www.electricdragonland.com

To Nana

Contents

Tattoo-Worthiness: An Introduction

I got a tattoo five years ago. I was speaking in Maui, had some time to kill before my flight went out, and decided to go to the Jimmy Buffet bar in Lahaina. There, across the street was Skin Deep Tattoo. And in my suitcase were the Chinese symbols that I'd been carrying around for months. It was time.

As Spike was permanently injecting ink into my virgin flesh, I asked him this question: What is the most requested tattoo? What do you think? Mom? Nope. A flower? Nope. Harley Davidson. That's right. The most requested tattoo in America (according to Spike) is a company logo.

Can you imagine your customers being so loyal to you—so enamored with you—that they would tattoo your corporate logo on their arms? If you're chuckling right now, you need this book. Harley did not set out to be a popular tattoo. The company has a loyal community of like-minded people that gather voluntarily to share their love of an idea. Oh, and it makes a decent bike too.

As you'll see in this book, becoming tattoo-worthy has less to do with product and more to do with listening and knowing your target intimately. It's the little things that build a brand. And the loyalty to that brand starts with the company—when you have a truly successful brand, it belongs to the customer. If you want them to be loyal to you—you have to be loyal to them.

All good business books have a list. There's the *7 Habits of Highly Effective People*, the *22 Immutable Laws of Branding*. And, even if the number is not in the title, you better believe there's a list somewhere in the book.

Apparently, we can't learn without steps. Look to the classic—the 12-Step Program originally developed for Alcoholics Anonymous. These 12 Steps may very well have begun our obsession with numbers and change. To honor the time-tested tradition of numbering the path from point A to point Z, I give you the five steps to becoming tattoo-worthy:

1. Target an Audience—Not a Territory

Some of you may think this goes without saying. But I grew up in the credit union world. You may or may not know this, but credit unions *were* founded by a group with a common bond. Credit unions began as a financial cooperative owned and operated by their members. The most common bond was that of employer. The oldest credit unions in the nation were formed by railroad workers, teachers, postal employees, and large corporations like AT&T and IBM.

Tattoo-Worthiness: An Introduction

Times have changed and so has the arena of financial services. The most recent incarnation of the credit union industry has witnessed the expansion of credit unions from their original targeted fields of membership. It has become more common to see a credit union increase its reach to include an entire regional community—territories, if you will—and literally attempt to target that entire area.

The problem with this approach is that in any given community there are such a variety of unique needs that you cannot possibly meet them all. So, if your business plan directs you to be the "best whatever" in your five-county region, you're crazy.

The concept of targeting an audience meets with so much resistance. When I ask my audiences, "who does Starbucks target?" people who don't get it will usually answer "coffee drinkers." Starbucks serves coffee, to be sure. But they don't target "coffee drinkers."

Starbucks targets me. I'm writing this introduction in a Starbucks right now. I have a bottle of water and a chocolate-dipped macaroon—yum.

But no coffee. I bought the water because the chalkboard sign behind the cashier said that the proceeds go to help children in third-world countries get clean water. I support that.

There's not a person in here that is not working on something. It's the middle of the day and people are reading in overstuffed chairs, or they're surfing the net on laptops, newspapers are strewn about, projects are being completed. We are all enjoying the "third place." According to Starbucks corporate philosophy, the first place is your home, the second is your office, and the third place—as Howard Schultz, Starbucks guru, discovered on a trip to Italy some 30 years ago—is the café.

Starbucks built an entire brand on this concept. In fact, they have done such a phenomenal brand-building job, they have made my top eight list—I know how you love numbers—of most tattoo-worthy companies.

2. Listen to your target

I've read several books advising the reader to *not* listen to the customer. Listening to your existing customer will not breed innovation. It can only result in incremental improvements to your existing product or service.

And, for the most part, I agree. Your customers generally don't have enough big-picture perspective to properly guide your company through major changes. So, instead of asking your customers, "How can we improve our business," ask them "What's up? How's your day going? What would make your day better."

At some point, the hotel industry became mired in the commodity zone. That is to say, very little differentiated one hotel from another besides the cost of a night's sleep or the size of a bar of soap.

Then the Internet exposed the hotel market. Suddenly, anyone could compare the prices and amenities of all the hotels at once. Websites were then developed to facilitate the comparison of hotels. As a result, the hotel industry had to scramble to come up with some truly unique differentiators—besides bigger bars of soap—to build customer loyalty.

Instead of panicking into some rash money-making decisions, the Westin Hotels and Resorts took some time to investigate the options. It listened to the target audience—business travelers—and asked them what the most important thing was in the hotel experience. Most people think it's speed at the check-in, or friendliness and cleanliness. They would be wrong. The number one thing the frequent business traveler wants is a good night's sleep.

The Heavenly Bed (as you'll read later) is an example of a company not only listening to its target but really responding to a need. Overachieving, if you will. And the bed, it truly is heavenly.

3. Know the competition for your target

Question number one: Are Dunkin Donuts and Starbucks competitors? I say no. Even though Dunkin Donuts has definitely stepped up its coffee offerings, even though it recently added Internet access, you will not catch me hangin' at the local D.D., writing this book.

Starbucks has a big fluffy couch. Dunkin has hard pink-seated booths. Starbucks has soft skin-caressing lighting. Dunkin has fluorescent. Starbucks has croissants and scones and marionberry bear claws from a local bakery. Dunkin has, well, donuts. Starbucks plays Joni Mitchell. Dunkin doesn't have music—that I've ever been aware of. Starbucks has ceramic, city mugs that I actually collect. Dunkin has an over-sized brown and pink travel mug, coveted by truck drivers across the nation.

So who *is* the competitor for Starbucks? Barnes and Noble could have been. But someone was smart. I'm not sure who initiated that relationship, but there's a magnificent lesson to be learned. About forming alliances. Once you've figured out who your target audience is, form an alliance with someone who is targeting the exact same audience but is *not* a competitor. The type of folks who go to bookstores will frequent Starbucks.

It was a natural then for B and N to partner with Starbucks and offer coffee, a place to hang, and wireless Internet.

The real competition for Starbucks is the local coffee shop. But unlike Wal-Mart—infiltrator of small towns and destroyer of "mom and pop" shops—Starbucks has managed to coexist with the local coffee shop. The folks who have never tried Starbucks may go once out of curiosity. If they like it, they'll go back. If they don't, they may not. They may instead decide they are morally opposed to big business, and choose to patronize the local coffee shop—rather than The Man.

If Starbucks is packed, I'll get my fix at the local coffee shop. I've been in some amazing joints. If they're doing it right, they *reek* local. Local artists adorn the walls. Local treats adorn the pastry case. These places specialize in something—like homemade pineapple upside down cake—and the baristas get to know everyone. By drink *and* by name. That's knowing the competition for your target audience. And there's room for everyone.

4. Make the competition irrelevant

Now that you have listened to your target, and know your competition, make your competition irrelevant. There is no better example of this than iPod. As you'll read later in this book, the folks at Apple hit a home run with iPod. The game is theirs to lose at this point. As I write this—I just

Googled the stats—iPod owns 97 percent of the MP3 market. How in the world did that happen? Apple was not first to market (which is usually a competitive advantage). Instead it was best to market.

Apple has had its ups and downs. But Apple inspires a cult-like devotion in its users. Being in marketing I was always surrounded by these "cult" members, Mac users who, even in the early days, were content to be different. The Apple customer is convinced that, because Apple is so good, there is no competition.

The great thing about Apple is it didn't set out to be the dominant MP3 player. It just followed a successful business model of focusing on usability. Being the best just followed naturally.

What a concept: make it easy to use and visually fun. Did you know it takes longer, in the world of computing, to make things easy for the end-user? It's faster and cheaper to make a series of incremental changes. Think record albums to 8-track to cassette to CDs. Incremental improvements to portability and durability. Remember what would happen when you left a record album on the sunny back seat of your Pinto? Or punched the same track on your 8-track player one too many times? Or got cake batter in your cassette player (maybe that was just me)? Even CDs can get dirty and scratched, and eventually your favorite songs start stuttering.

The digital music file was a gigantic leap forward in music portability. But Steve and the gang were brilliant in forming an alliance with music distribution companies. So you didn't just buy a device—you entered a new world.

iPods have truly disrupted an industry. If I owned a record store today I would be nervous. Since I got my iPod, I have not set one foot in a record store. I'll probably never buy a CD again—in a package. Now I purchase

my music online, one song at a time. It's cheaper and quicker, sure. But even better, my iPod, it just looks cool.

By being true to and listening to its target, iPod has made the competition irrelevant.

5. Be loyal to your target

This goes out to all of the executives at GM. I'm a very loyal Saturn owner. I have purchased four of them in four different states, had them serviced at six different locations, and I am fiercely loyal to your brand. Don't screw it up in the name of profit. If you do, I'm outta here. And your profits *will* dwindle.

As you'll read later in this book, I am devoted to my Saturn. Not necessarily the car, but the company. Which just recently was—gosh, I don't even know how to say it—*reassigned?* to the big, bad boys at GM.

GM owns Saturn (on paper). Always has. But what truly makes Saturn unique is its independence from this huge company.

Saturn was an experiment of sorts. When US auto sales were sagging miserably, an executive at GM convinced the company to let him start a "different kind of company" and build a "different kind of car." The result: one of the highest-rated cars ever for customer satisfaction and repeat business.

The Saturn brand oozes customer service and Saturn-community inclusion. Saturn makes me feel spoiled and loved. And that's the trick when you're that good: maintain loyalty to those who bought in to your brand in the first place. Don't lose sight of what makes a customer loyal—it's not the car, it's the experience.

Tattoo-Worthiness: An Introduction

Avoiding alliances with the wrong competitors, knowing when to say *no* to big money because it flies in the face of being loyal to your target, it's no easy task.

The Blue Man Group is a perfect example of that. They started as three guys in the streets of New York City who had a unique form of art, combining music with skits and no speaking. They took their show on the road—literally—and now perform all over the world. The shows are true to their roots. They do evolve with the times, but what the Blue Man Group won't do is sell themselves out to corporate America.

Naturally they've been approached to endorse a number of brands, but the only one they accepted was Intel. Why Intel? Because, with Intel, the Blue Man Group managed to maintain 100 percent creative control over the ads. And, as a result, the ads are fun and brilliant.

How many of us could say no to millions of dollars in the name of our brand? If you want to be tattoo-worthy, you need to learn how.

There's your list. It's a down and dirty description of what I have come to believe about attaining and maintaining a successful brand along with—the all-important—brand loyalty. If you don't read any more of my book, I think you'll still walk away with some nuggets to ponder.

If you do read on—and I think you should—I hope to mildly entertain and, more importantly, drive home the point that anyone can be tattoo-worthy.

Denise Wymore
August 10, 2005

1 *The Westin Heavenly Bed*

s I write this I'm on a plane to Chicago O'Hare. Just another day in the life of the business traveler. It's post 9/11 so you can imagine what I've been through to just get in this seat. Up at 5 a.m. Feed Puss Kitty. Make some coffee, shower, finish packing. Check emails, verify flight departure time. *Again.*

Onto the express lanes of Seattle's I-5 by 6:30 a.m. for the 17-mile commute to the Master Park Lot C. Onto the shuttle to the terminal. Up the escalator to the United counter. Shamed into using the E-Check-in machines (even though I'm 100K Executive Premier). Machine spits out the boarding pass. Wait for my name to be called, present my luggage (under 50 pounds). No, it's not locked (for the thousandth time), and no, there's no film in it. Proceed to the security line. Get in the shorter one because (did I mention?) I'm 100K Executive Premier. Show my ID and my special pass.

Shoes off. Coat off. Laptop out. Purse in bin. Coat and shoes in bin. Laptop in bin—all by itself in its *own* bin (you'll only make that mistake once). Computer case on belt after bins. Wait to be summoned. Slowly (but not too slowly) walk through metal detector—or whatever it's set now to find. X-Ray machine spits out bin number one—grab the laptop. Bin number two, throw coat over my arm and shoes on the floor in front of my feet. Try to wiggle my toes in the openings as I stuff my laptop back in the case that the machine just spewed out. Metal rollers twirling their happy sounds—glad to be free of yet another business traveler's stuff.

Down the escalator to the train to take me to the "N" gates. "Please hold on," is spoken in four different languages. Whoosh to the N Gates. Doors open, belch out the travelers as another herd waits to be sucked in. Up the escalators, one last stop in the gift shop for water and a magazine. Onward to gate N-14.

Find a seat that has at least two empty next to it. Business travelers are especially picky about the seats in the waiting area. It is considered very bad form to sit directly next to someone if you can avoid it. I guess this is our last chance at some kind of personal space. Once we get on board, all bets are off.

Group number one is called. You scan the folks in line, wondering who you'll sit next to. Praying it's not the harried mom with the screaming toddler. Down the jet way, wait for the first class passengers (who were given early boarding so they could get their stuff settled) to continue getting their stuff settled. To the Exit row.

Ahhhhhh.

I'm only 5 feet, 4 inches tall. But I'm 100K Exec Premier (did I mention that?) so I can get the Exit Row, if it's available. I can climb over sleeping seatmates to visit the little girls' room without touching them—usually.

In my seat. Pull out the latest edition of *Distraction Magazine* to endure the plane-loading experience. I used to enjoy watching people board until I realized how much I had grown to hate them. Now I can't stand to watch people ignore the pleading of the flight attendants. "Please step into the aisle and let the 357 passengers still standing in the jet way behind you get to their seats so we can make an on-time departure and not have to spend three hours in Chicago rerouting the 249 passengers who missed their too-tight connections because you had to fold up your raincoat gently and place it on top of your briefcase that should be under the seat in front of you!"

So I spend the next thirty minutes trying to escape what's happening around me by reading about Jennifer Aniston's metabolism or Julia Roberts' latest marriage. And pretending to read the safety instructions—since I *am* sitting in the Exit Row, after all. I verbally say "yes" to the flight attendant's question so she can verify that I speak English. Really. This just started recently. You have to respond to her with a verbal yes. Apparently this verifies that you do speak English. Yes. How many languages can you say "yes" in? Just curious.

Finally. Lift-off. And then come the onboard menus. Gotta decide if you're going to pay money for a meal that's been sitting on the tarmac for the better part of a day—or take your chances with the "snack" that has been prepared by the anti-Atkins high carb/high sodium junkies industry. And can I please have the whole can of soda and not the partial cup-full that I share with someone in seat 27-A?

Seat belts fastened, tray tables in their upright and locked positions, seats up, shoes back on. All carry-ons safely stowed, laptop computers and all other electrical devices, including walkmans, iPods, and gameboys, must be turned off. We are beginning our initial descent into Chicago. Taxi to the gate. Wait for the ding—up, bins open like popcorn in an air pop, a shower of overhead luggage coming down, narrowly missing strangers' heads. Stand in line, ignoring all personal space now because we are near an end.

Every city I've visited I like to play this game. I don't look at the signs above to see the baggage claim area. I just assume that the mass will take me there. And they always do. Somebody listened on the plane as we were welcomed to the city du jour. Rookies.

"Airplane travel is Nature's way of making you look like your passport photo."

-Al Gore

Let's talk about personal space again. If travelers were to stand at least six feet back from the luggage carousel and not approach it until their bag is in sight, no one would get hurt. But people have to stand with their knees touching the metal for fear that they won't be right there when their black roller bag comes by. I, however, always stand back at least six feet. I hope to start a trend.

Here comes my bag. It's not black, it's taupe (which is always a hard color to describe to the airlines when they lose it). It has a big yellow Mickey Mouse luggage tag. No matter how loud or how often I say, "Excuse me," the wall of luggage grabbers is not likely to part like the Red Sea for me to get my bag. So I push, I pull, I fling, I grunt. I'm on my way to the taxi line.

There are two kinds of taxis: smelly and barf bucket-smelly. There are clearly no laws or standards of cleanliness for this form of transportation. I have to go to my happy place to endure it. Or, if it's really bad, straight to the shower when I get to my room.

Onward to the hotel. First I must pay the cabbie. Always have to ask for a receipt which is either handed to me blank (with a few extras, wink wink), or it's handed to me blank and looks like something that had been photo copied in the '80s.

Bellman usually offers to take my luggage at the Westin. I always say "No." It started as a feminist thing. *I don't need no stinking bellman to carry my things.* Then, when I actually did say yes, I had to wait almost half an hour for him to deliver to my room. That does me no favors. I like to get settled as soon as possible. And waiting around is like waiting for company you dread. The house is already clean, you're just sitting in the front room trying to look natural—don't get up to pee because that's when the bell will ring.

Now I check into the hotel. Always, always, always, be nice to the front desk clerks at a hotel. They hold the power to your comfort. There is absolutely no reason to ever get testy with these folks. Smile. Ask them how *their* day is going. They know how yours is—you just spent the better part of it standing in lines, sitting in the most uncomfortable chairs, and riding in smelly cabs, all on about three hours of sleep.

It doesn't hurt to compliment their hotel and the city and to explain that this is your first visit and how excited you are. I swear this gets you a better room. Really. So you get your plastic keys, directions to the elevator—one more chance to hand your luggage to a stranger, and pay extra to bring it up 30 minutes later—and you're off.

Ding. Your floor. Look again at the room number written on the folder. Up at the arrows and numbers on the wall. And down the hallway. Odds on the left—evens on the right. I should be on the right in three, two, one more door. Key in. Arrows down. Green light comes on. Whoosh.

Moment of Truth. SNIFF. I asked for non-smoking—appears I have it. Light switch on. Halogen lights click and blink to life. Wheel in the luggage.

And there it is:

The Westin Heavenly Bed

Its king-sized mountain of cootie-free white linens and pillows rivals the display beds in Macy's. The cloud-like comforter has a subtle chintz stripe of white against the 400-thread-count stripe of fine Indian cotton. You dare not put your grungy suitcase on this mountain of fluff so you quickly search for the luggage rack.

As you go to hang up the outfit—the one that has been cooped up in the bowels of a 757 for hours that you have to wear to speak before an audience of 200 in the morning—you notice the heavenly bath robe. It's displayed on a satin hanger with its sleeves tucked into the pockets as if to say, "Look at how cool I am."

Then I dump my Ziploc bag full of exploding gel and lotion and toothpaste onto the marble counter of the Westin Heavenly Bath. Embroidered white Egyptian cotton bathsheets are draped on a black lacquer stand poised over the commode. A glass shower stands in the corner with two giant showerheads that promise to soak you from head to toe without your having to move at all. And a glistening white porcelain tub with slanted back and lovely, scented bath bubbles. A washcloth folded like a napkin rests next to the shower. I truly am in heaven.

Or so I think.

The Perils of Commoditization

So, how did the Westin come to spend upwards of $3K for each bed in its hotels and still manage to remain competitive on price? Here's what I know: Westin Hotels and Resorts is really in the service business. Its target audience is the upscale business traveler. Me. That means people who travel for companies with budgets that can afford a little nicer hotel. Westin then competes with Hilton, Hyatt Regency, Ritz Carlton, Sheraton, and Marriott. What do they all have in common? Well, everything. A beautiful lobby. Bellmen. A concierge desk. Nicely appointed rooms with beds, hairdryers, desks, sometimes a mini-bar. You get the idea. So, how do they differentiate themselves?

Some try with the bathroom amenities. I've been to a hotel that boasts Bath and Body Works and Aveda products. I've also conducted my own personal research and concluded the size of the bar of soap is in direct proportion to the cost of the room. Motel 6 gives you a sliver of a wafer that, if it doesn't crumble when you release it from its wrapper, will surely mysteriously disappear somewhere in the shower with your first use, while the "W" hotel in Chicago gives you a huge, lovely bar of soap—and a view.

With the differences between upscale hotels being minimal, Westin executives decided to ask me, the business traveler, "What do I seek in a business hotel? They did a ton of focus groups. They asked me what it was like to travel. I told them what I just told you: *It couldn't suck more.* Most business travelers agreed that they didn't sleep well on the road. Westin asked why. We told them:

- *The beds are uncomfortable.*

- *There are never enough pillows (and they are mostly those hard foam ones.)*

- *You don't want to even sit on top of the bed for fear of cooties from those painfully gaudy bedspreads. And when you finally build up the courage to check out the blanket beneath, you are usually welcomed with the errant cigarette burn on the acrylic blanket. Eeeek.*

- *The showerheads are usually those bullet, water-conserving sprayers.*

- *The bath towels smell like locker room towels, are small and itchy, and they're way too small to wear around the room.*

One, quite frankly, can't wait to leave. And the hotel industry has accepted this for the most part, recognizing that it is, after all, a rented room.

But at the Westin, customers *rave* about sleeping in the Heavenly Bed. They didn't want to get up in the morning. They had the best night's sleep.

But here's where it breaks down. Brand must ooze from every pore of the organization—the Westin almost gets this. The marketing of the experience is some of the best I've ever seen. As best I can tell, they have a brilliant marketing team that has partnered with some Martha Stewart-like decorator[1] to bring the Heavenly Bed concept to everything you touch.

For example, the DO NOT DISTURB sign is not stock. It has a picture of a man on one side and a woman on the other sleeping in the Heavenly Bed. It simply reads, "Can't come to the door right now, I'm in Heaven."

The towels in the bathroom have a silver label that says "Heavenly Bath." Their colors are white and silver. The colors of clouds. The soap is wrapped in silver. The labels on the shampoo and conditioner are very plain with silver lids. Very minimalist—very clean. Nothing says clean like white.

And the best part—you can buy the Heavenly Bed. (There's a brochure on the nightstand.) I just met a guy on a plane who did. Cost? *$3000*. Amazing.

Managing Moments of Truth

So, the Westin did a great job differentiating themselves *in the room*. See, a bed is a thing. So is a sparkling tub, and a delicious bathrobe. And *things* are reasonably easy to manage with money and a modicum of upkeep.

However, the Westin comes up short in a little department I like to call *Managing Moments of Truth.*[2] For now, this is what you need to know. Managing things, easy. Managing people—and all the *needs* of those people—hard.

---

1 By the time this gets published Martha will have already worked in the kitchen at the State Pen, but you can't deny it, the woman can decorate a room.

2 More on that later.

The Westin made a valiant attempt with a concept they called SER-VICE EXPRESS. I can just see the meeting where this concept was born. Continuing to build on the *sanctuary* concept, Westin opted to simplify the in-room process by building all requests into one simple key on the phone. No more squinting at the buttons to see which one directed you to *wake-up call*, *room service*, or *front desk*. Now, with SERVICE EXPRESS you simply press *one button* for any and all of your needs.

Sounds great, right? The problem with the SERVICE EXPRESS button is that it usually rings and rings and rings. I would say, on average, I can't get a person to answer 50 percent of the time. At that point, I'm really *searching* the phone for the other buttons—but there are none. Not even on the side or bottom. I checked. Should you find yourself with a real emergency on your hands, your *sanctuary* moment can quickly turn into a nightmare. You'll know what I mean by this when you read the last chapter. Don't peek—read all the stories first.

Frosting on the Pig

I've met so many talented graphic designers who can make a bar of soap look like it should be in a museum. Super Bowl commercials have gotten so good that I now watch the game so I don't miss them. Whoever thought that we would watch a 60-minute special dedicated to commercials? There are award programs and publications honoring the best in print, radio, and television advertising. But the truth is—none of this builds brand. It merely entertains us.

Brand is built with the experience. Brand is the emotional connection you have with the company—not its commercial. The Westin Heavenly Bed is just frosting on the pig. The *real* moment of truth is in the rest of the experience. Think about it—my first impression was amazing. This big pile of fresh white fluffy love that extended to the bathroom and the soap and truly oozed from every pore of the organization. But every time I hit the SERVICE EXPRESS button, it's like hearing a needle scratch across a record album. Ignored, abandoned, alone. I guess that *is* an extreme definition of *sanctuary*.

I've never stayed at a Ritz Carlton. Frankly, I'm a little afraid to—I've heard so many awesome things about them I don't want to be disappointed. I want to believe that *they* have it all figured out.

Unfortunately, the Westin isn't quite there. The *sanctuary* brand—successfully represented by the Heavenly Bed, Heavenly Bath, and Heavenly Bathrobe—does not ooze from the receiver of my SERVICE EXPRESS phone. As soon as I put my ear to the sound of that incessant ringing on the other end, my moment of truth, my *belief* in the brand, is obliterated. To restore my faith, and the faith of all the other business travelers who seek *sanctuary* at the Westin, the business of that *sanctuary* must be practiced like a religion[3]. But so many organizations fail to do this.

Since the time when Westin introduced its Heavenly Bed, no doubt so has every other hotel in their category. Here's the problem with a commodity-type business: R and D. Rip-off and Duplicate. The Sheraton now has their own version. So does the Marriott. I even stayed in a fairly swanky Holiday Inn recently that boasted Tempurpedic mattresses. The Heavenly Bed is no longer a differentiator. But, alas, it is easier to manage.

At my last visit, the SERVICE EXPRESS was still anything but.

---

3   *For more on that subject, you should enjoy the next chapter. The chapter my friends said I shouldn't write.*

DO
NOT
DISTURB!

The Westin Heavenly Bed: Five Steps to Tattoo-worthiness

1. **The Target Audience.** *How did the Westin hotel do? Definitely targeted an audience, the business traveler.*

2. **Talking to the Target.** *They talked to them. They listened to them.*

3. **Knowing the Competition.** *Every other high-end hotel chain.*

4. **Making Them Irrelevant.** *They set out to make them irrelevant. Sadly the bed could not sustain that difference long term because it is so easily copied. For the Westin to truly make the competition irrelevant, they have to build on the SERVICE EXPRESS. Well, first of all they need to actually make it work. They need to meet my minimum expectation—and that would be to have someone actually answer the phone.*

5. **Staying Loyal to Their Brand.** *Where the Westin can really separate themselves from the pack is in step number five. Be loyal to your target. In other words, keep talking to us. Find out what else would make our lives easier and then wow us. A perfect example of this is wireless high speed internet. I just checked their website again to make sure they still have not figured this one out. They have not. They do offer high speed internet access. But they charge for it. This is so not being loyal to me. Even Holiday Inn gives it (internet access) for free. So add it to the cost of my $200 plus a night room—I'll never know the difference and have it be "complimentary".*

The Westin Heavenly Bed is tattoo-worthy.
Sadly, the hotel is not—yet.

2 The Catholic Church

The Experience is Everything

y earliest memory of being a Catholic involved my mom grabbing doilies out of the glove box of our Mercury Comet station wagon and bobby pinning them to my head.

God, that hurt.

It was 1967—before Vatican II. Women had to cover their heads to enter church. If that were still the case today, I'll bet little 10-year-old girls would be wearing their baseball caps—backwards. *Word.* Were lace doilies ever in fashion as head wear? Or was my mom just viciously complying with an age-old doctrine? Frankly, I'm surprised she didn't just drop our cat

Cinder on my head and tell her to hold on.

And so it was. Every Sunday we would march into church. The good Catholic family with five kids. We always sat in the same pew, as if it had our name on it.

Several years later I learned that I was a sinner. I was in the process of preparing my sinful soul to receive the sacrament of communion. Communion is given every Sunday in the Catholic Church but only those who are free of sin are allowed to receive it. Here's the deal. We are all born sinners. Except for the Virgin Mother (she was conceived without original sin; For more on this, see The Truth about Immaculate Conception.)

Since it's not really cool to say that an innocent little baby is filled with sin, Catholics perform the Sacrament of Baptism shortly after birth. In the Catholic baptismal ceremony your parents are supposed to appoint a Godfather and Godmother. It's not necessary that they be married (although I think they prefer that.) The role they are supposed to play is that of your *Guardian of Christ*. That is to say, bear witness to your being baptized and be in your life to make sure you stay sin-free. Parents can only do so much.

My parents apparently didn't read the brochure so they appointed their friends Joe and Allana to be my Godparents. They played bridge together almost every Friday and shared a love for martinis. My Godparents are now divorced. Today, Joe is a Moonie in Seattle and Allana is an alcoholic who treats rehab like summer camp. I think she's been five times.

THE TRUTH

e celebrate the feast of the Immaculate Conception on December 8, the day before Donny Osmond's birthday. Okay, he's Mormon, but I always remember that day because of him. Most people think the Immaculate Conception refers to Mary being a Virgin when she gave birth to Jesus. No, that was just one[1] of God's many miracles. Here's the real definition according to a great website, http://www.catholicmom.com/immaculate_conception.htm:

On December 8, we honor Mary, our Mother on the Solemnity of the Immaculate Conception of the Blessed Virgin Mary (a Holy Day of Obligation). The doctrine states that "the Blessed Virgin Mary, in the first instance of her conception, was preserved exempt from all stain of original sin by a singular privilege and grace granted by God, in view of the merits of Jesus Christ, the Saviour of the human race." To read the Church's doctrine on the Immaculate Conception, visit Catholic Encyclopedia's article. To send a Catholic e-greeting commemorating the feast, well, there's a place for that too. Anyway, I've won many a bar bet with that little tidbit. Now you can too.

By the time a Catholic is about eight years old, it is assumed that he or she is a sinner again. I guess baptism has a shelf-life. In the second grade I was preparing for the Sacrament of Confession so that I would be worthy of the Sacrament of Communion. Turns out there are two types of sins. Big sins—mortal sins—that you can reference those in the Ten Commandments. Then there are more minor, or venial sins, which I think nuns make up, depending on the rowdiness of the class. A venial sin, according to Sister Annette, is lying to your parents, taking a toy from your sister, cheating in a card game, and, of course, the one you learn later—swearing. These don't necessarily break your friendship with God, they just piss him off. Mortal sins, however, do break your friendship with God until you receive the Sacrament of Penance. But at eight I was hard-pressed to come up with a sin worthy of confessing. Even a venial one. So I used to make up sins. When I explained this to Sister Fidelis, she told me I must be lying and in so doing, I had sinned.

Well, there. That takes care of that. Now I could proudly go to my first Confession. So I entered a dark, little room, smaller than any closet in my house. I knelt on a wooden plank and waited for the sliver of light to appear in front of me indicating that the Priest in the closet next door had opened the gates for me to recite my Act of Contrition.

We are all sinners, remember? I mean, I'm in the second grade. What have I done at that age that condemns me to hell? Oh wait, I lied.

And so the guilt party begins. If you think about sex, you're a sinner. If you have sex before marriage, you're a sinner. If you marry, divorce and marry again *and* consummate the marriage—you guessed it—you're a sinner. So, thankfully, there is *weekly* Confession (and the opportunity to receive the Sacrament of Penance). See the pattern?

After you confess your sins to the Priest, he gives you Absolution and a Penance. The Penance is supposed to be directly related to the seriousness of the crime (*er, sin*). If you lied to your parents, you get about two Hail Marys and an Our Father. Cheated on a test? Might get you ten Hail Marys and an Our Father. I'm curious about what sin might get you a whole Rosary— just to test this "weighted" judgment thing. I know I've committed them but never really had the courage to admit it. But I do say a Rosary now and again just to make sure I'm not destined for eternal damnation.

Even though I now consider myself to be a recovering Catholic, I really wouldn't trade the experience for anything. The education I got at St. Mary of the Valley Academy School for Girls was first rate. But the thing I have grown to appreciate the most from the experience was just that—the *experience*. The experience of weekly mass, the experience of tradition, and the experience of Catholic doctrine.

Why Corporations Need a Values Filter

I said earlier that I believe that corporations don't have values, people do. I also think that corporations are like families. And, like families, a ton of them are dysfunctional.

Speaking of dysfunction—my family was in that boat. And not just because we were Catholic. We had the usual five kids, my mom had to work, my dad loved to drink—pressure from his job as the quality control manager for the local nuclear power plant—you know the drill.

But my parents did have a values filter, whether they knew it or not. The decisions they made—good or bad, conventional or not—were based on what they valued and on how they were raised.

One day, the values of my mom were broadcast to the family, loud and clear, when she put our house up for sale. We had moved from Southern California to a cute little town called Aloha, Oregon. I never did find out why it was called that. My mom liked it because, although it was a mere ten miles from downtown Portland, it was still in the country. We had horses and cows and a filbert orchard on our street. It was a time and place where kids would ride their bikes for miles just to go to the store for ice cream, and could camp out in the front yard without fear of being kidnapped, and you could leave your front door unlocked—at night. It was a lot of fun growing up there.

Then one day, the filbert orchard, just, went away. It looked like a horror film—flat, dusty debris as far as the eye could see. Seems Intel had bought the farm, literally, and was going to build the first of many Pentium chip manufacturing plants.

So that day, my mom announced we were moving to the city: Portland, Oregon. She said she was tired of watching our cute, little town turn into a city, so her objective was to move us somewhere that was already built up.

Without a values filter, a family (now picture it as a business) might just sell their current house for top dollar and go buy the biggest house they could get in the city for the same price. But *with* a values filter, there are several issues that must be taken into consideration when making that new purchase.

My parents had five kids and at least two pets at any given time. And we were Catholic. Very Catholic. The ideal home, therefore, would have to have a yard, at least five bedrooms, and be within walking distance of a Catholic church (and a Catholic school). So, that's exactly what my folks got. It wasn't easy to fill that criteria based on our budget, but with time, research, patience, passion, and drive, miraculous things can come to fruition.

Businesses make decisions all the time with only the bottom line as the values filter. If your only measure is profit, you most likely are eroding your culture with each new venture. When is big enough going to be big enough? Never. Because bigger does not mean better—*better* is better.

Practice Your Culture Like a Religion

Ultimately, brand is about repetition and practice—you must practice your brand as you would practice your religion, telling your story over and over in everything you say and write, produce and create. People hire me all the time to motivate and energize their staff—for one hour. As in a religious service, I can definitely lift spirits for an hour. But then what? A business must continually motivate and energize each and every week to make it matter. To make it stick.

The Catholic Church understands repetition and practice.

- *It has all these great rituals. Every Sunday at church the gig is the same. Stand up. Sit down. Stand up. Kneel. Sit down again. Walk up for communion (if your soul is in a state of grace). Back to your pew. Kneel. Sit. Stand. And we're out in sixty minutes—on the dot.*

- *It is completely obsessed with the repetition of symbols. The Catholic Church definitely has the most recognizable logo in the world. You can go to any Catholic church anywhere and find they are pretty much laid out the same. An altar, with the logo hanging prominently behind. Holy water dispenser to your right. Pews with kneelers. The distinct smell of candles and incense. The stations of the cross—six on each side. The novena candles. The donation box—à la the Starbucks tip jar.*

- *It understands the importance of telling the story. Sunday Mass tells the same story every week. Literally tells the same story, over and over and over. And over. The only time it changes, even slightly, is for the Big Days—Christmas and Easter. Between Sundays you're supposed to "practice what is preached." And by the time you die, you're supposed to have gotten it right. That is the point of "practicing a religion." I finally get it.*

Like it or not, your company culture is also your company's religion. Company culture and religion both function according to certain predominating attitudes and are characterized by certain behaviors. If you want to build a sales or service culture, it's not going to be done in a single meeting with a follow-up memo. Or worse, in *four weeks* of training where everyone practices new skills within a controlled environment and then—*boom*—is expected to have created a perfect, little sales and service culture. If only it were that easy.

Ultimately, organizations do not have values—people have values. And the companies that have successful cultures, cultures that can withstand the test of time, are the companies who live the values of their leadership.

totally-catholic.com

God I love this world—and of course I kind of just sinned right there by starting that sentence with "God" and not using it as praise. Damn. Oops, there I go again. Anyway, I was just surfing through the catholicmom.com site and it led me to www.totally-catholic.com. So here's another moment of truth. Catholicmom.com did something right because when I Googled the "Feast of the Immaculate Conception" she was right there on the front page. Then, after reading her definition, I couldn't help but wonder what kind of movies she recommends—being the good Catholic that she is. But, before I could even click on that, I noticed a link for totally-catholic.com. You can totally buy totally cool Catholic T-shirts. The sad thing is—and here's how they are NOT managing moments of truth—half of their website's links (no, I mean to say all but one of the website links) are broken. When you click, it just says, "Coming soon." Disappointing. I see that they have visions for the future, but rather than show me all of those closed doors, just put up a totally cool, totally catholic T-shirt web site. Once you've figured out the rest, put that up too.

Now I know what you're thinking. The Catholic Church has had some pretty scary things happen lately—priests molesting altar boys, and the pope just died and was replaced by a very old German priest with rumors of Nazi connections. And just as scary, they are being sued all over the place and my own archdiocese in Portland has filed for Chapter 11 bankruptcy protection. Further proof that everything is a brand and that the Catholic Church is a business.

But they still do a lot of good. I wouldn't trade my Catholic upbringing for anything. I *did* learn right from wrong. I understand that sinning is bad and that hurting people is bad. I get it. I don't always practice them, but I definitely know the rules of the game.

Go forth and practice what you preach.

Believe, value, cherish, want.

The Catholic Church:
Five Steps to Tattoo-worthiness

Do I dare judge the Church's brand based on my list? Okay, but quietly.

1. **The Target Audience.** *Check.*

2. **Talking to the Target.** *Sometimes.*

3. **Knowing the Competition.** *Always.*

4. **Making Them Irrelevant.** *This would be an awesome thing to debate in a theology class.*

5. **Staying Loyal to Their Brand.** *With a vengeance.*

The Catholic Church is tattooed on my soul—for eternity.

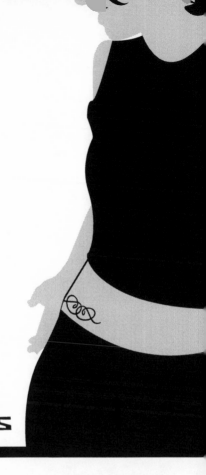

3 Craig Carothers

 It's a Saturday night in Seattle—and it's not raining. I'm sitting at my kitchen table, drinking a Manhattan, laptop up, wireless DSL connection, headphones on, and I'm glued to a webcast from a little-known spot in LA called the Kulak Woodshed. I sit for two hours at my kitchen table watching my favorite performer, Craig Carothers, play guitar and sing the smartest songs I've ever heard. Know why I did this? I have no life? Nope. I'm dating Craig? Nope. I just got DSL? Nope. I'm doing this because Craig sent me an email:

> Tomorrow night, March 27, I will be performing with my friend Randy
> Sharp for a live webcast from a place called Kulak's Woodshed, in
> Los Angeles at 8 pm PST. The address and directions for the physical

location can also be found at: www.kulakswoodshed.com I'm told that if you have a high speed internet connection it will be just like watching TV. On the other hand, if you have a dial-up connection like mine, it will be like watching a NASA broadcast from the moon. Either way, please tune in. CC

Craig did what most of us don't do. He asked for the business. But he didn't do it with a sign on a bus or a billboard. He's cultivated a community of like-minded people. Craig is not trying to be all things to all people with his music. He has a very specific target audience for these emails—Portlanders who love good food and good music.

The first time I saw Craig perform, it was a complete accident. About ten years ago I was out to dinner with friends. It was one of those perfect evenings. We'd had a fabulous dining experience and just enough wine to not want the

PHOTO BY DAVID WILDS

Craig Carothers photo appears courtesy of the photo stylings of David Wilds.

night to end. So we decided to go for a nightcap at Huber's in Portland, Oregon. Huber's is known for its tableside preparation of Spanish coffees. Big flames, big show, good stuff.

Well, there was a line out the door. And as we stood in the rain, feeling defeated, we saw a little place across the street that looked like fun. Al Amir, a Lebanese restaurant with a pretty cool bar in the front of the restaurant. In the back of the restaurant was an elevated stage about the size of my bathroom. Two guys were sitting on chairs, playing guitars. Butted up against the bar was an upright piano, with another guy playing. It was the kind of music that draws you in, not only because these guys were talented musicians, but also, because their songs were original and funny and clever without being stupid. A rare thing.

After ordering the Lebanese margaritas (don't ask, but let's just say, you should drink only one) we asked if we could move to the back room to better enjoy the music.

Craig is a big, burly man with jet black, wavy hair and a scruffy graying beard. Next to him was a guy wearing wire frame glasses and a beret on a head of graying, straight hair in a pony tail—Tim Ellis. On the floor in front of the bathroom-sized stage was an old, upright piano with a skinny, geeky-looking guy—Gary Ogan. If you want to really understand what an experience it was, you have to go to www.cdbaby.com and order The Craig Carothers Trio CD. It's the only one they did together. It's a live performance. It's magic.

Craig takes his audience from seriously beautiful contemplative tunes like *Day at the Beach* to a rousing rendition of *Petticoat Junction*. If I were a singer, I would be Craig. He doesn't play it safe with potentially commercially successful tunes but rather tells his story through snappy lyrics and incredible strumming. Craig does not dress to impress. He is as genuine a northwesterner as they come. In fact, he was wearing navy blue sweat pants and a Hawaiian shirt the first time I saw him. He's a big guy. He's a lovable guy. The kind of guy that you want to drink beers with in your backyard.

I began to frequent this bar. It was the kind of place that you'd bring out-of-towners to. Great food, incredible music, and no cover charge.

One of the best ways to build your brand, according to my friend Dr. Lynda Falkenstein (author of the book *Nichecraft*), is to align yourself with people who are going after the same target audience but are not your competitors. In Craig's case it would be a radio station called KINK and a tavern called the Buffalo Gap. If you're ever in Portland, you need to check out both.

Kink is 101.9 on the FM radio dial. KINK's promise (tagline) is to be "True to the Music." That means that they will play literally any genre of music if it's good. And that would be KINK's version of good. Not that of the record stores, or Hollywood's, or Casey Kasem's. During any given hour, you could hear the Rolling Stones, Lee Ritenour, Bonnie Raitt, LeAnn Rimes and, of course, Craig Carothers.

Craig Carothers

Craig began a tradition in Portland called Songwriters in the Round[1]. He convinced a little bar called the Buffalo Gap to let him invite Portland songwriters to play *sans* microphones. It was to be a true gift to the audience. On those nights, the Buffalo Gap ceased to be a bar and was instead transformed into someone's living room. That was Craig's vision.

I heard Craig on KINK radio one morning plugging the event. He basically told the listeners that if they wanted to go to a bar and socialize, don't come to the Buffalo Gap. This was a performance, not background music, and because it was totally acoustic, if you did come and talk, you would get the stink-eye from all of those around you.

I decided to experience Songwriters in the Round for myself. It was one of the most intimate, incredible experiences in which I have ever participated.

I took piano lessons as a kid. From a nun. Recitals were a necessary evil. No one dared speak during one. The audience was there to honor the student's achievement; everyone was rooting for the performers. And they heaved a collective sigh of relief after each victorious achievement—followed by thunderous applause. That was Songwriters in the Round: Craig's brainchild, created to enable local talent to showcase their material. It was brilliant.

A couple of years ago Craig moved to Nashville, Tennessee. At first it broke my heart, but eventually I understood. Nashville is the music capital of America. And that's where Craig began to really cultivate his brand. Craig had a loyal group of followers. He knew that. Craig embraced technology and simply began staying in touch with us via email. Whenever he came back to Portland, I'd get an email. Short, sweet, and to the point.

I've been able to get my fix of Craig periodically since he left. I got an

---

1 *Held at the Bluebird Cafe' in Nashville, www.bluebirdcafe.com.*

email that he'd released a new CD—it directed me to www.cdbaby.com. A
Portland company. I bought it. Got another email from Craig thanking me.
I also got a world-class email from CD Baby when they shipped the music.
Check this out:

> Your CD has been gently taken from our CD Baby shelves with steril-
> ized contamination-free gloves and placed onto a satin pillow.
>
> A team of 50 employees inspected your CD and polished it to make
> sure it was in the best possible condition before mailing.
>
> Our packing specialist from Japan lit a candle and a hush fell over
> the crowd as he put your CD into the finest gold-lined box that
> money can buy.
>
> We all had a wonderful celebration afterwards and the whole party
> marched down the street to the post office where the entire town of
> Portland waved 'Bon Voyage!' to your package, on its way to you, in
> our private CD Baby jet on this day, Saturday, February 28th.
>
> I hope you had a wonderful time shopping at CD Baby. We sure did.
> Your picture is on our wall as 'Customer of the Year'. We're all exhaust-
> ed but can't wait for you to come back to CDBABY.COM!!
>
> Thank you once again,
> Derek Sivers, president, CD Baby
> the little CD store with the best new independent music
> phone: 1-800-448-6369 email: cdbaby@cdbaby.com
> http://www.cdbaby.com

Now *that's brand!*

Once again, Craig has aligned himself with people as cool as he is.

I have never met Craig. Never spoken to him. If I walked past him on the street, he wouldn't even know who I was. But last night, we connected for the first time—via the webcast. I tuned in and was glued to the grainy image on my laptop.

The woodshed site invited me to email the artist during his performance. I did. I requested he play *Little Hercules*—his first hit from the '80s. He did. I sent another email reflecting on my experience:

> Craig
>
> Never thought on a Saturday night I'd be sitting at my kitchen table on my IBM ThinkPad with my wireless high speed, headset on, glued to the webcast of your concert. Must be like color television was in the 1950's... we're making history baby.
>
> Denise Wymore
> Portland, Oregon Fan

I sent it while Craig was singing and when he was through, he read my email to the audience. They even showed the computer screen of the email! Keep in mind, I'm watching this from my computer in the kitchen—on a Saturday night. What a rush.

Then as the concert continued I noticed this on the homepage:

> Help keep the Kulak's Woodshed webcast alive. Please participate with your financial support. Please make a PayPal contribution. (The more people watch, the more Kulak's Woodshed has to pay. Our current monthly bill is $1,600.00 just for the webcasting streaming bill alone.)

I have a PayPal account. So I sent $50. At the end of the song, Craig read my email again. And thanked me for the money. I got an email today from the owner of the Woodshed thanking me for my support.

When is the last time you thanked your customers for their business?

Brand is an emotional connection, just like a relationship. We have something in common. Brand is about asking for the business and following up to make sure everything went as promised. Brand is about thanking people.

Craig Carothers:
Five Steps to Tattoo-worthiness

1. ***The Target Audience.*** *Craig does all five right. He targets an audience.*

2. ***Talking to the Target.*** *He doesn't market to everyone in Portland, he wants people who enjoy listening (not talking during) music.*

3. ***Knowing the Competition.*** *He has no competition.*

4. ***Making Them Irrelevant.*** *He has made the irrelevant*

5. ***Staying Loyal to Their Brand.*** *he's been extremely loyal to his target. He simply makes the effort.*

I would tattoo Craig on my neck.

4 Saturn

y first car was a 1973 VW Super Beetle named Howard. I loved that car. I learned to drive in that car. One day Howard died a horrible death and left me stranded on the side of the road. It was one of those times when you realize it's cheaper in the long run to buy a new car than to resurrect the old one. Poor Howard. It was time to say goodbye.

At the time, I was working at Portland Teachers Credit Union, so I got pre-approved for my first-ever new car loan. I convinced Bill, my (now) ex-husband, to go shopping with me on his birthday (because it happened to land on a Saturday—not my fault).

Nothing could have prepared me for the awful experience of purchasing a new car. Where did these car dealers go to school—*Hell?* You pull up to the car lot and they're lurking by the front door, smoking their cigarettes dressed in raincoats. Hair slicked back, clip-on ties. As soon as your foot touches the pavement, they're on you. Apparently you can't just "look" at new cars; you have to endure their incessant chatter about how they're going to "put you" into a new car today.

I test-drove a Honda Civic—nice car. The sticker price was darned close to the amount of my pre-approval. So we went into the office to begin the negotiation process. The salesman immediately led us to a room in the back with no windows and a metal desk with matching metal chairs. It smelled like an ashtray.

I presented my pre-approval letter, as instructed by my credit union, to act as a shield against the evildoers. It didn't even faze him. He left us in the room for some time—apparently to go negotiate with The Devil himself to see if he really could get me in this car. The salesman finally returns to inform me that unfortunately there's a $300 discrepancy with our offer. That is to say, I'm willing to pay X and he wants me to pay Y. I refuse. I get up to leave. He relents, "Okay, I see what the problem is. You don't have enough money. Do you have any guns or jewelry you can sell?' Amazing. Guns or jewelry? Excuse me—am I in Texas? (Not living there yet—but see chapter eight for more on that.)

We left the Honda dealer the same way we left Subaru and Nissan—dazed and confused. "Where to now?" Bill asks.

Well, my brother Carl, a *Consumer Reports* nut—won't buy toilet paper without consulting their latest poll—had just bought a Saturn. He proceeded to quote me their customer satisfaction ratings, fuel efficiency, along with a myriad of other virtues. This was 1990 and there was but one dealer in the entire Portland Metro area selling Saturns at the time. We were disgruntled and disillusioned, grubby and exhausted.

What had we to lose?

We arrive at Saturn of Beaverton, and at this point I just want to get in—look at a car—and get out if I don't like it. I have no idea what a Saturn even looks like. Check it out—we literally hunkered down and shuffled between the new cars to avoid being pounced on by the dealers. Down one aisle—up the next.

Then I saw her—Buttercup. And she was loaded! Keep in mind, I drove a '73 Beetle for years, so my expectations were pretty low. I really just wanted a defroster that didn't involve a rag from the glove box. Buttercup had a defroster (now standard), and a sunroof, and power everything, and she was the cheapest car we'd looked at all day—well within my budget—*and* she didn't have one of those "We'll hose you, cuz we can" additional dealer markup stickers on her. I popped up from my crouch to reveal myself to the potential pouncers.

You know what?

No one came.

I looked around.

Not a lurking, smoking, slime ball to be found—anywhere.

I walked up to the building—there were people in there—and stepped through the doors. Immediately, I was greeted by a nice young lady, "Welcome to Saturn. What can we do for you today?" (Um, I don't know—knock me over with a feather?)

"Yeah, I'd like to test drive this car out here," I replied. So the nice-young-lady buzzed the back room and out walked Eric.

Cool guy. Smelled good. Dry handshake. All his teeth. The kind of guy you're not afraid to get in a car with.

As we're test-driving Buttercup, I'm thrilled—I had found my car. And I'm not afraid to say it. Bill, starts squeezing my leg so Eric can't see and is giving me the sideways stink-eye. "What?" I seethe. Oh yeah, the second largest purchase you'll make in your lifetime—and you're supposed to pretend you don't really like it. He's gearing me up for the negotiation process. We will have literally no power at all if we let on that we actually *want* this car.

As we pull back into the lot, Eric jumps out of the back and turns to us to say, "Do you have any questions about the car? If not, I'll leave you two alone so you can spend more time with it and talk privately. I'll be in here if you need me." Amazing. We could have gotten away. Just walked on out of there without incident.

Naturally, I followed him right into the showroom and shouted, "I want to buy that car." Gulp. We were escorted not to some scary back room, but to a sitting area right out there in the middle of the beautiful showroom. Eric began by saying "At Saturn, we don't dicker on the sticker. We feel that we've priced our cars fairly, and that's not how we want to begin our relationship with you." Whew. I'd been "negotiating" all day and quite frankly didn't want to play that particular mind game anymore either.

What a novel concept—price your product fairly. Hmmmm. Maybe that will catch on.

I showed Eric my pre-approval letter. Great. Now we just need to fill out the paper work for the DMV. He gathered our information and showed us a cozy little waiting area. Nice couches, a television, chick mags. But the best part of this wait was when Eric surprised Bill with a birthday cake and a balloon! They must have noticed on the paperwork that today was his birthday. To this day, I will never know how they did it—I wish I'd asked—but somehow I just like to savor the magic of it all. I'm busy thinking, "whew, one less thing I have to worry about today." In the midst of my car-crisis, I had forgotten to bake Bill a cake.

When it was time to sign all the papers, we were escorted to the F & I guy's office. He began by asking us, "How has your experience at Saturn been today?" We're eating cake. Um, I'd have to say it's been pretty darned good.

I doubt very much that the F & I guy at the Honda dealer would've had the guts to ask us what we thought of the experience. Can you even imagine how that would have gone?

Did our sales people do any of the following:

1. *Pounce on you the moment you entered the lot? Check.*

2. *Chatter incessantly? Check.*

3. *Make you feel scared and alone during the negotiation process? Check.*

4. *Insult you with inane questions about assets that you could sell in the alley to scrape up just enough cash to pay too much for an average car whose value will drop 33 percent the moment you leave our lot? Check.*

5. *Drive you out of the dealership without making a purchase and prompt you to write a book about how shitty the experience was? Check.*

Meanwhile, back at the Saturn dealership, while we were in the office signing all of the paperwork, they had pulled little Miss Buttercup into a section of the showroom.

No car will ever look better than at that moment. There's something about the lighting in the showroom. It's like your diamond ring in the jewelry store—it makes every inch of you sparkle. They asked if they could take my picture with my new car. I tried to restrain myself from lying across the top like a super model (thought it might scare them.) They showed me all the features and cool stuff in the trunk. And then they opened the doors to the showroom, handed me the keys, and as I drove away, all the available salespeople stood around clapping—just like in their old commercials.

Wow.

That night I was still amazed at how great that experience was and said to Bill (a credit union CEO) "Man, if a car dealer can do that—why can't a credit union?"

Why do people accept the humiliation of the car buying process? Because no one else was doing it any better. I've heard that some other dealerships now have the guts to price their cars fairly, doing away with the dicker-on-the-sticker madness. I know there will always be a market for the negotiators. That's fine. Some people just like to argue their way through purchases.

Remember, Eric told me that the reason they don't dicker on the sticker is because it's not how they want to begin our relationship. They meant it. We were beginning a relationship. One that has lasted almost 15 years. A month after taking Buttercup home, I got a calendar in the mail from Saturn. It featured my picture with Buttercup. In between the month pages were coupons for cool Saturn stuff and service discounts. At 3000 miles I took her in for her first oil change. When I went to pay and pick her up, I was told

that my first service on my new Saturn was their "gift to me." Didn't cheapen it by saying it was free. What woman doesn't love gifts? A free oil change and "our gift to you" are two entirely different things in my heart.

My car had been washed, vacuumed, and there were two chocolates on the dash with a thank-you note. Nice.

After I'd had Buttercup for a year, I received a card in the mail. On the front it said, "Honk honk. Beep Beep." Inside it read, "We wanted to wish your Saturn a Happy Birthday in the only way we knew it would understand."

Now how damn cool is that?

Every time I've taken my car to Saturn for any kind of service I've been delighted. Not just satisfied but downright thrilled. It's the little things. For example, they made a note in the computer that I'm one of those whack jobs who names her car, so when I arrive for service they ask me what Buttercup is in for today.

I'm now one of those warranty-crazy people. I love the peace of mind that comes with warranty. Consequently, I've been trading in my cars about every two years or so, depending on the new colors and models that Saturn has to offer.

The second Saturn I bought was in Eugene, Oregon. We had moved down there, and one day as I was in the dealership for an oil change. I noticed the beautiful, blue, two-door sport coupe in the showroom. Had to have it. Since I am now a loyal owner, I knew the drill. The process was so painless and so fun—I couldn't wait to see what I would get with my second purchase. Not only did I receive the great no-haggle process, but this time they had a gift basket for me with a Saturn travel mug, umbrella, stickers, and chocolate.

The third Saturn I bought was in Seattle, Washington. The new SUVs had just come out. By this time you could shop on the Internet and I *knew* their website would be as cool as their showroom. It is. You can go online and build your very own Saturn and then find a dealer and go pick it up. I seriously did this. I built a beautiful Saturn VUE online, and clicked on the dealership in Lynwood. Got an email back from a salesperson immediately with a few questions. Got a call an hour later telling me I was approved for financing and could she *deliver* the car to me that night? Wow! I had a meeting that night and I kind of wanted to go to the dealer for the whole show. So I told her I'd come in the next day.

I walked in the showroom to meet Linda. And while they were paging her I saw a big *yellow* VUE!! They didn't have yellow online. You have to know this—I'm obsessed with the color yellow. Not taxi cab yellow, though—which lots of cars tend to be. Daffodil yellow. This VUE was daffodil yellow. As Linda walked out and saw me drooling over Tweety she said, "You must have the yellow one. Am I right?" Yup. "No problem," she said, "we'll just change some paperwork."

Tweety was moved to the end of the showroom (so I could drive her out) and she was decorated with tons of yellow balloons. In the windshield it said on a big card—Denise's new car! Doesn't that just give you the chills?

When I tell this story in my speeches around the country, I usually get someone (a white male, for some reason, in his late 50s) who is rolling his eyes and gasnorkling. I don't blame him. He probably thinks a) I'm an idiot and b) all that stuff is stupid. And he's right. He's right to feel that way because Saturn is *not* targeting him. At all. They are targeting *me*. A woman who names her cars, who is emotionally driven, and who will be as loyal as the day is long if you buy her gifts and shower her with love. And it doesn't take that much. A thank-you card here. A yellow balloon there. A piece of chocolate. We're simple creatures. And our loyalty translates into *huge* profit for Saturn. That's why they do what they do.

As I mentioned earlier—a car is the second largest purchase you'll make in your life. I think the average new car, as of this writing, costs around $24,000. Many of you reading this have probably purchased a car by now that cost more than the first house you bought. We're talking a lot of money.

Imagine, then, that I make this huge purchase once every two or three years? Wouldn't it be nice for a dealer to know that I'm going to keep coming back? I'm not going to stray at all? My loyalty to the brand is so fierce that even the news that General Motors (the parent company of Saturn, incidentally) has recently decided to "take over" management of its little darling did not keep me from buying Saturn number four.

This year I got an apartment in Northampton, Massachusetts. I sold my VUE to the Lynwood Saturn for a very fair price and bought a new one at Saturn of Hadley. My salesperson was brand new, and I wanted the ION four-door, burgundy with tan interior, and it *had* to have a sunroof. This kid called all over to find exactly what I wanted and drove to Boston to get it. I didn't have a car so he delivered my paperwork to me, took me to an insurance person and to AAA. Then to the dealer to get in my shiny new car. They had the nice little waiting area with good coffee, television, and more chick mags. When my car was ready, the nice clean, service guy came into the waiting area to show me all they had "performed," pointed out the window of my shiny, clean car (inside and out), and told me that the keys were in it, engine running, ready to go.

The beauty of my Saturn experience—are you listening corporate General Motors fat-cats?—is that it was consistent, for 15 years in four different states. That kind of stuff does not just happen. That's building a culture and practicing it like a religion (see *The Catholic Church*, chapter 2).

Saturn has an incredible culture—the company was funded, you could say, by GM. It was the brainchild of a GM exec who wanted to see if treating people well worked. Saturn's promise is to deliver a different kind of car from a different kind of company. Their brand oozes from every pore of their organization. Rather than build their plant anywhere near Detroit, they went to Springhill, Tennessee. They wanted no one from GM to build this company. To really change a culture, sometimes you have to kill it off and rebuild. They had a separate union contract. They empowered every person on the line. They wanted to not just build a good experience, but a quality car as well. So anyone at anytime could stop the line if he or she felt the quality was compromised in any way. Unheard of in the car business. They have "daily devotionals" at the dealerships. That is to say they celebrate their culture (the salespeople do not work on individual cut-throat commissions but, instead, as a team.) Everyone shares ways to wow their customers and they have fun doing it.

Saturn:
Five Steps to Tattoo-worthiness

I'm very happy with my ION. But I have to admit, I am a little worried about the future of Saturn. GM executives have already announced that they are going to discontinue the manufacturing of the polymer side panels on all new Saturns. Brilliant.

I didn't even mention much about the cars—other than they are consistently highly rated in Consumer Reports for reliability. If you go into any Saturn dealer (and you'll have to go quick—they may already be gone) there's a car that is partially ripped apart to show the safety features and to highlight the fact that you cannot dent the side of a Saturn. They invite you to kick, pound, go medieval on the side panels. They have this unique, rubbery plastic component that will not dent. I haven't had a door ding or an unfortunate shopping cart incident for 15 years. It was a clear DIFFEREN-TIATOR in the car. But, of course, it cost a little more to make, so GM cut it. Typical corporate stupid move. All in the name of profit.

If GM messes with the culture—that is to say if their bad juju erodes the love that exists at the dealerships—I'm done. The cars are nice—but the real reason I'm so loyal to Saturn is because of the experience. The accountants at GM probably don't get that. How do you quantify the experience? How can you prove that it matters? It's tricky.

I hope that someone out there is taking the time to see that I've purchased four of these cars. Do the math on the profit. Send me a thank-you.

I'll be back.

1. *The Target Audience. Saturn did have a clear target audience. Women.*

2. *Talking to the Target. By listening to them challenged the age-old process of dickering on the sticker. Women overwhelmingly said they don't want to do that. Price the cars fairly and we'll buy them. Give us a flower, a birthday card and a thank you and we're loyal for life.*

3. *Knowing the Competition. The competitors for their target were many. And this is why I hope that the history books will at least acknowledge the project.*

4. *Making Them Irrelevant. When the Japanese were clearly kicking our you-know-whats an American car manufacturer (GM no less) starts a whole new car company. And it succeeded. They made their competition irrelevant by delivering the basics—a good quality car—and then really exploring the relationship. Their goal was "repeat business." Recognizing that the company could make more money by treating people well, pricing the cars fairly and following-up with stellar maintenance.*

5. *Staying Loyal to Their Brand. The real test for Saturn will be step number five. If you google "Saturn" and "experience" you can see how they've made a difference. Saturn owners are fiercely loyal. To the dealers and the mechanics. To the experience. Will GM have the guts to be loyal back? Time will tell.*

I would tattoo Saturn on my left shoulder. One of those tattoos that doesn't hurt as much to get and, let's face it, really only shows in the summer or in the shower. But still I would put it on my body. It's a great story.

5 STARBUCKS

ot *another Starbucks story!* I know—not a business book in
the last quarter of a century is doing its job unless it men-
tions Starbucks. So I have to. Sorry. I love them. I've written
most of this book in the Starbucks on Lake City Way in Seattle. It was so nice of them to take this old Denny's-style building and convert it into the most comfortable place for me to sit and write.

They put in this nice, desk-type table with cobalt blue lamps. And
there's an outlet on the wall behind me so I can plug in. It was even nicer of
them to become a T-Mobile Hot Spot so I can check my email while I work.

I just ordered the grande mint mocha chip frappuccino for $3.70. I will
sit here for at least two hours. If Starbucks were a bank they would prob-

ably think of a way to discourage my business. Like charging me for the electricity I'm using. Or put in some kind of rule that you cannot use the desk unless you spend at least $10. After all—I'm loitering. I'm taking up quite a bit of real estate for $3.70. So how does Starbucks make any money? The answer—they positively know what business they are in.

My 23-year-old nephew, Matt, is a manager at a Starbucks in Hillsboro, Oregon. I asked him what his training was like when he started with the company. He told me that the first thing you learn about is the "third place." The third place is a concept that Howard Schultz—a Starbucks marketing manager who later bought the company—brought over from Italy when he convinced the owners of Starbucks to try out the coffeehouse concept in Seattle in 1989. In Europe, the first place is your home. The second place is your office, and the third place is the café or pub where people "hang." In Italy, these cafes not only serve excellent espresso, they also serve as meeting places or public squares; they are a crucial component of Italy's societal glue. At the time, there were 200,000 of them throughout the country.

That's the basic model for the Starbucks store. To be a gathering place. Matt told me that his job as manager is to protect and promote this third place. As I'm sitting here, an employee is outside scrubbing down the tables and cleaning the windows. Another employee is picking up discarded newspapers and putting them in the community bin and then fluffing the pillows on the brown velvet couch next to me.

Some people argue that Starbucks coffee is not that great. They could be right. Howard Schultz believes that they are not in the coffee business serving people. They are in the people business serving coffee. That's why they've converted to automated coffee-making machines while investing time, money, and energy into developing the atmosphere of the stores.

Starbucks subscribes to the theory of five senses merchandising. When you walk in, they hit them all.

- *Sight: soft lighting,*
- *Sound: their own brand of music compilations,*
- *Smell: what smells better than brewing coffee?*
- *Touch: At most stores you can fondle the beans, the Barista Bears are yours to hug, and there are mugs, finger puppets, candies and all manner of fun stuff to pick up, turn over, and purchase, and*
- *Taste, of course: it's all about customizing the drink to fit your taste.*

No one pays better attention to this than Starbucks. They have written standards for their coffeehouse experiences. That's why they are brilliant with their branch strategy. Whether it's a little hutch in an airport or a café in a Barnes and Noble or a stand-alone store, they look, feel, sound, smell and taste the same. Starbucks does not believe in franchising. They fear losing their consistency.

Today, Starbucks has 9,481 branches. I've visited Starbucks in France and Australia and Canada and Hawaii and just about every state in the US that has them. They all "feel" the same. I am their target audience. They expect me to hang out for $3.70. And they expect me to come back and to buy their music and subscribe to their XM Satellite radio station (number 75) and to buy the occasional Barista Bear and to begin collecting their city mugs so I can show off to my houseguests how many cool places I've been.

That's how Starbucks makes money. They get brand. They are passionate about it. It oozes from every pore of the organization. They practice it like a religion. And they make a ton of money doing it.

Starbucks:
Five Steps to Tattoo-worthiness

1. *The Target Audience. NOT coffee drinkers. I ask audiences this all the time. If you were thinking that, maybe I've not been clear. Truly tattoo-worthy brands go beyond their product. Starbucks and Dunkin Donuts. Are they in the same business? They serve basically the same products, but I would argue their target audiences are different. Starbucks is targeting creative thinkers and Dunkin the daily commuters. Good debate topic. Talk among yourselves.*

2. *Talking to the Target. Proof number two that Starbucks does it right and Dunkin is practicing R & D (rip-off and duplicate). Because Starbucks listens to their target, they were first with wireless internet. I mean, really. What does that have to do with coffee? Nothing. It has everything to do with the type of people they cater to. DD on the other hand has added wireless internet to some of their outlets back East. It's just sad. I mean who wants to hang out in a formica topped table in a hard wooden chair under fluorescent lights? Might as well go to a bus depot—same ambiance.*

3. *Knowing the Competition. The real competition for Starbucks is not Tully's or Seattle's Best (which Starbucks now owns) or Caribou. I think it's the independent single coffee shops in anywhere USA. They now have the opportunity to connect even more with their audience because they are local and should know them more intimately than this huge company from Seattle.*

4. *Making Them Irrelevant. I don't think Starbucks has made the little shops irrelevant. But I do think they will always be the leader of the chains if you will.*

5. ***Staying Loyal to Their Brand.*** *Here's where Starbucks has to be careful. Even though they don't franchise per se. They are aligning themselves with grocery stores, airports, and book stores (Barnes and Noble to name one). It's been my experience that these places are not run with the same zeal as the real stores. In fact, the employees at many of them are downright rude. And the cleanliness is never guaranteed. I was thrilled the first time I saw a Starbucks in my grocery store. But there are times when I just cringe for their brand. Employees are chatting, the place is a mess—an entirely different experience than a store run by corporate. This is where I think Starbucks has the biggest opportunity to kill their brand. Getting too big.*

**I would tattoo Starbucks on my left hip—not for public display.
Just my own private nod to their greatness.**

6 iPod

I can hear a song and go back to a date and time and I swear in my mind I see vividly the people, the place; I can smell things, I can feel things—all triggered by a song.

I remember the first time I spent my own money to buy music. I was in the fourth grade and I bought a 45 of the song *Dizzy*. My folks had one of those console stereos that was a beautiful piece of furniture with fabric on the speakers and a lid you opened to the turntable part. You made sure the knob was turned from 33 1/3 to 45, and after we lost the spacer thingy we had to use our fingers to line it up straight. And you could never get it exactly straight, so when you set the needle down it was like jumping rope. You'd have to visually follow the rhythm of the movement and then, set it down (jump on in). *Dizzy*. That song was mine—I literally owned it. That began my obsession with music.

My first album was the *Partridge Family Sound Magazine*. That's when I first learned that there are songs on some albums that just shouldn't be. I would never admit it to anyone at the time, but I found that quite a few of the tracks sucked. Of course, in the days of record albums, to change a tune was an ordeal so you just stuck it out.

My first concert was during my freshman year of high school—a boy named Roy Rogers (I kid you not) asked me on a date to go see Wild Cherry (the one-hit-wonder that brought us *Play that Funky Music White Boy*). Normally I wouldn't go out with someone I didn't really like, but hell, I'm 15, I've never been to a concert, and that song was hot. Roy also brought beer in his Pinto—I think he stole it from his parents. He had three cans of Schlitz Malt Liquor, still suspended from the plastic rings, on the floor in the back seat. He wanted me to help him *slam them down* before we went in.

These were the days of festival seating, which meant you had to get in line and push your way to the front. I declined the Schlitz and am instead standing in line, holding our place, while Roy is in the car *slamming them down*, and then he comes back up to me and says, "I've gotta pee." Um, yeah. So he strolls a few feet away to a parking lot that is separated from us by a thin row of hedge. You guessed it: my date peed in public on our first (well, lets be honest, our only date). But the concert rocked—and I was close enough to the stage to touch the lead singer's hand. I was hooked.

There's nothing like live music. On my 21st birthday I saw Phoebe Snow perform at what is now the Roseland Theatre in Portland, Oregon. That was my first experience with the lounge atmosphere. That is to say, they serve you drinks while you experience the music at your own little cocktail table. You don't have to slam them down in the parking lot before—but I bet Roy is still doing that today anyway.

My favorite concert—the Rolling Stones. Johnny Lang opened for them when he was only sixteen years old. The Stones were all over fifty when I finally could afford to see them—but I have to say that heroin has been good to Mick. That man can move and don't get me started on Keith Richards. Scary? Hell, yeah. But he can play the guitar like no other in my opinion. So, for some reason, I was drawn to him. I mean, seriously, I had a freaky little crush on him for awhile.

I got free tickets to see K.C. and the Sunshine Band when they were just about to fizzle out—guess who opened for them? A band that had quite a following but was not yet commercially successful. They were called Santana. What an experience! I had never, ever heard music like that, and as soon as K.C. and the boys started shaking their booties, my friend Julie and I looked at each other and said, "let's go!" We just couldn't bear to undo the greatness buzzing around in our brains that was Carlos.

I've purchased a ton of music in my life—from albums to cassette tapes, and was an early adopter of the CD. But I never quite understood the MP3 concept. I wasn't a Napster when it was technically illegal. I just bought bigger books for my CDs so I could travel everywhere with my music. I tried like hell to find a CD player you could jog with that didn't stop or skip. Tapes were okay but they were so linear. So, naturally, I took the time to make compilation tapes. I started making them for my runs—and had the perfect one for the time I ran the San Francisco Marathon. I knew it would take me about five hours to finish, and I didn't really want to hear the same song twice. I needed certain songs at different times so I made three compilation tapes. After tape number one I was getting tired so I flipped on the radio. I didn't know any stations in SFO so I started flipping and there he was: Dave Matthews performing live in the studio of KFOG. What a treat. I listened to Dave for about two hours—this is when I became Dave's groupie—and when the show was over, I went back to the tape.

It was a grueling thing, the marathon—I don't think anyone is meant to run 26.2 miles[1]. I had carefully planned my last song—it had to be Carly Simon's *Let the River Run* (remember the last song in the movie *Working Girl*—when Melanie Griffith calls her girlfriend to let her know she's no longer working for the man—she IS the man.) Anyway, an awesome song and I have to admit, I wept when I crossed the finish line. Partly because I was in so much pain, and partly because that is one perfect song. So, of course, if ever I need a lift—need to go back to that moment—I put it on.

If you're a music junkie like me, then you know that you can get yourself out of or into any mood with music. I have the pity party series for lost loves. Then there's my angry chick music set. And the meditative new age spiritual set. There's head banger time. And the classical/opera genre for cooking with a glass of red wine. Good stuff.

One day, my best friend and favorite business partner bought me an iPod as a gift. That iPod changed my life—the iPod was made for me. I am truly their target audience.

---

1 *And let me tell you, that last 0.2 is a bitch. Because, at mile 26, there's a big sign that says "26" but you're not done yet. You still have 0.2 to go, and that's just mean.*

First of all, it is visually stunning. It's small and sleek and white and clean. The back is all chrome and my friend even had it engraved with my name.

Remember making compilation tapes for a boyfriend or girlfriend? I made one as recently as 2000. All music junkies had a time in their lives when they had to express themselves through compilations. I own very few movies—but *High Fidelity* is one I have for that very reason. It's all about the compilation. Before I owned a lot of music I used to hang by the radio and wait for my favorite songs to play—one finger poised over the Record button, the other over the Play button. Those early compilations always had this rip noise at the beginning and end of each song—but it was okay because you were doing something cool. And I thought it should be illegal for a disc jockey to ever talk at the beginning of a song. To this day that drives me crazy. I'm always thinking "What if some kid is at home trying to make a compilation tape, you insensitive twit!?"

When my dad graduated to a stereo receiver, I could make my compilations from actual albums, and it would record all the scratches and hisses and skips. Then we did cassette to cassette and, if you could do that, it meant you probably also had a feature called high-synchro dubbing—which meant you could completely copy one cassette quickly onto the next. If you turned up the volume it sounded like the Chipmunks. Then CDs came along. Now a compilation tape was so much easier....and Bill Gates had the vision—he didn't invent the iPod, but he predicted it in his book *The Road Ahead*—if a CD could be made, why limit it to being burned on what looked like a small record album?

Basically the music is digital—so you should be able to transfer that file to a computer or put it on the Internet. And thus the iPod was born.

I manage my music collection on my laptop with iTunes. I simply pop in one of my CDs into the drawer, and iTunes identifies all the tracks—time, title, genre—and loads them into my library. When I plug in my Pod, it automatically synchs it up with the library. So, here's the part that is so freaking awesome. You know that song I didn't like on the *Partridge Family Sounds Magazine*—well actually there were several—you just uncheck 'em in the library. It takes them off, so you will never have to listen to a song you don't like.

Compilations. Are you kidding? This bad boy is all about the compilations. The entire iPod was built so you could build your own and it would track what you really listen to. I just checked my own Top 25 most played. Very revealing. I'm vacillating between angry chick and rock star mode right now.

I will never buy another CD again—because I can go out to the iTunes store and buy songs for a buck. Any song for a buck—so let's do the math. *Jagged Little Pill* has 13 songs on it—that's 13 bucks. But if you hate *Forgiven*, like I do, it's only 12 bucks. That's a cheap CD. Now that I've transferred all of my music onto the iTunes, I'm tempted to pack all my CDs up—I'll never play them again because I bought the iPod docking station and stereo connection. So, literally, my three shelves of CDs are now held in a device that's smaller than my TV remote. I could buy a bunch of candles and tchotchkes to put on those shelves!

There are games on the iPod—if you want to play while you play. There's solitaire, of course, but there's also a name-that-tune music trivia game that takes five of your loaded songs, displays them, and then plays a portion of just one. You race against the clock to choose which one it is. Now how smart is that? And how fun? Wouldn't you have loved to be on the committee that came up with that one? It had to be built by music lovers. And that's one of the problems with most brands—the builders are not the target audience. They have no idea what they really want. So they guess, or worse yet, they try to please everyone on the committee—you've no doubt heard that the camel was a horse built by committee?

Anyway, the greatest thing happened last week. I was in Massachusetts with the friend who had given me my engraved iPod. We were praising the power of our iPods, when he pulled out his iTrip. The iTrip is a little device about the size of a chubby tootsie roll that pops onto the top and acts as a transmitter to your FM radio. How cool. The only problem is, you have to find a station that has nothing on it—and in a big city that's pretty hard to do—so we found one with minimal static and put on some Led Zeppelin, marveling at the technology that is the iPod. The irony? We couldn't get really good reception so there was tons of static—but we didn't care. It was more scratchy than an LP—or a slightly loose melted cassette, or a CD that jumps and skips—but it was a great band. Rock on!

iPod:
Five Steps to Tattoo-worthiness

I'm a button pusher. I'm the annoying person at Best Buy who accidentally hit the "screaming volume" button on the demo stereo. I don't like to read manuals. Most of them were written by Satan anyway.

The iPod was so easy to figure out. I've never in my life owned an electronic device that was so intuitive. The more I learned about Apple I understood why that was. The entire company is committed to the user experience. It may take longer to get the product to market but it works and it's a thing of beauty.

Since I came from the corporate world, I was a PC user. Network Nazis hate Macs. I think it's a job security issue. With a PC you have to configure and setup and decipher the simplest of things. Like adding a printer to a desktop. With Mac, you just turn that bad boy on and it talks to you. My home is all wireless. Network back-up, printers, internet. My husband had to configure all this for my old IBM ThinkPad (ironic name, huh?).

Then I came home one day with the PowerBook G4. Flicked it on, and boop.....we have a new sheriff in town. Wanna play in this network? Sure, I say. I'm in. It's that simple. Freaks out the network boys. I'm a Mac cult member now. I like to go into the Apple stores and just smell stuff. I'm making movies, playing with digital photos, in general just being a creative little genius. All because my Mac encourages me. PCs will "let" you if you can figure it out.

1. **The Target Audience.** The type of person that made compilation tapes and took the time to write the song's name AND the length of the song on the cassette cover.

2. ***Talking to the Target.*** *It's all about usability. And how cool it looks. Their target audience requires both.*

3. ***Knowing the Competition.*** *Here's where Apple ended up owning 87% of the market. The mp3 market was, for the most part, making incremental improvements to the portability and durability of the previous innovation (the CD). The players were still too linear and too cumbersome. iPod came in and made a player that was fun, funky and easy. It is all about the compilation. You can make a "mix tape" in about two minutes.*

4. ***Making Them Irrelevant.*** *One word. iTunes.*

5. ***Staying Loyal to Their Brand.*** *I've heard some iPod owners say they felt Steve sold out when he introduced the BLACK U2 iPod. Time will tell if Apple can be commercially successful (finally) and stay loyal to their cult members.*

I would tattoo the Apple logo on my ankle. The outside of my ankle.

7 CHICO'S

I am five feet, four inches tall. My ancestors are German. My mom used to joke that when she gave birth to me, I "crowned" twice. Once for my head and a second time for my calves. I haven't worn a size six since junior high school. Some might say I'm "big boned." Whatever. Doesn't mean I have low self-esteem or a poor body image. I just hate shopping for clothes but I *love* clothes.

Fashion is just mean. The year I turned forty those damn low-rise pants were back. I was in the fourth grade the last time they were mainstream popular. I had a pair of ducky yellow ones that buttoned up the front and I looked pretty darned good. Today? Not gonna happen. I have the opposite of a low-rise figure—No waist and a flat butt.

So now I'm destined to wear "mom-jeans." You know the kind. They come up over your belly button and, to get them comfortably around your waist, they sneak in a strip of elastic so the two chunks of love on my hips poof out. Lovely.

I stopped tucking in my blouses when I lived in Dallas. One of my book club friends pulled me aside one night and gently said in a sweet southern drawl, "Honey, after we turn forty, we stop tucking in our blouses." But my boobs are so big that, if I don't tuck, I run the risk of looking pregnant. The most depressing thing that could ever happen to a woman would be for someone to ask when you're due—and you're not. Not that being with child is a bad thing (so I've heard) or that pregnant women look bad (they don't). It's just that you don't want to appear to be so large that someone assumes there's a human inside your belly.

I have no idea what color my hair is. I haven't let it be that color for at least ten years now. I suspect it's got some grey in it by now. And there's really no reason whatsoever to let that happen. I really started playing with color about five years ago. Currently I'm sporting a look that my sister affectionately refers to as the calico cat. Gives you some idea of the chances I'm willing to take. But the point is, when I started playing with my hair, I realized that I could no longer wear my preppy Catholic schoolgirl duds. You know the look. Khaki pants, polo shirt in the summer, button-down oxford in the winter, penny loafers, socks, and the essential navy blazer. This was my look for years. Eddie Bauer was my store. But once Blockbuster Video employees adopted "my look" I decided I might need to crank it up just a bit.

I went to Nordstrom, reluctantly. Now don't get me wrong—I love Nordy's. Customer service is among the best, and the no-hassle return policy is amazing. I walked in the store one day, took a six-month old shoe off my foot, and handed it to the shoe guy to take a look at something that was poking up in the heel and making my hose run. I really just thought he could fix it for me. To my eternal amazement, he presented me with a brand new pair *and* directed me to hosiery for a complimentary pair of replacement hose! That's good stuff. But I'm not really Nordstrom's target audience. I'm neither rich nor thin enough. And there's something about buying Nordstrom clothes that makes me nervous. The pieces seem fragile to me. You have to dry clean almost everything, and most of the styles are very tailored.

A couple of years ago I was thumbing through the Nordstrom catalog and noticed a whole new selection of flowy, earth-mother clothes. A lot like Coldwater Creek sells. Linen long skirts with big boxy jackets and big jewelry. And dresses out of a high-quality T-shirt fabric. I think they were trying to go a little more full-figured with this line. But I don't want to wear jackets that look like they could have been made from a quilt. For some unknown reason, I'm violently opposed to wearing anything patchwork. And as cute as some of the hand-painted palm trees are on these T-shirt dresses, they are still not me. Won't do it. I want a look that says I'm an artist, I'm a professional, and I'm just as much fun as my hair.

I was in the Denver airport making a connection when I spied this beautiful, black, flowy, long-sleeved dress with a black duster jacket over it in a little boutique called Pizazz. It was made of some kind of polyester fabric, but let's just say the black was jet black and the fabric did not look or feel like polyester but more like silk loaded with lycra. I didn't even have time to try it on so I just grabbed it—paid $150 for it and stuffed it in my carry-on.

When I arrived in Vegas and pulled this new find out of my bag—it was wrinkle free. As I placed it on a hanger, the little frock danced and glistened in the hotel light.

The next day as I slipped it on, I felt like I was wearing a luxurious silk nightgown. The fabric is amazing. It's just heavy enough to be a bit clingy and still be forgiving. And the duster gently covered any imperfections that may be appearing around the panty line. I loved this dress. I felt pretty, comfortable, sexy, and more importantly (since I was getting ready to speak before an audience), free to sweat. It met all of the criteria for what I like to call Speaker Clothes. Comfy. Flattering. Sweatstain proof. And as an added bonus, it could be machine washed without wrinkling.

This is the day that changed my life. Someone at the end of the session asked me if I was a "Chico's girl." I had no idea what that meant. "No," I said, "I'm not." "You sure do look like one," she added. Chico's is a women's clothing store, she went on to explain, and it has unusual clothing that not everyone can get away with it, but she felt somehow I could. I had to check this out. There was one in Vegas at the Aladdin Hotel.

When you enter a Chico's you are immediately drawn in by the color. Very, very seldom do they do pastel. It's all about vibrant, beautiful colors and the most amazing accessories. They also have the good taste not to use too many mannequins. I hate mannequins. Those skinny, little, plastic bitches that barely have the curves for a size zero. I've seen jeans pinned in the back of a mannequin to make them fit. Geez. Why do stores do this to us?

At the end of every rack, there is a complete accessorized outfit displayed on a system of hangers. So no matter how big or small you are, you picture yourself in it. The real you—not the overgrown Barbie doll at most department stores.

Chico's truly knows its target audience: Women of all shapes and sizes who want to wear clothing that is comfortable, artsy, and fun. It's the only place where I've seen ages 30 and 60 shopping side-by-side. To appeal to this broad a group, they questioned everything in the process of shopping for and trying on clothes.

First there is the sizing. They'll ask you (if you don't look like an obvious Chico girl) if you are familiar with their sizing. Here's how they explained it. Because sizes vary so much in fashion, they've simplified the system. They have four sizes: 0, 1, 2, and 3. Size 0 at Chico's does not correspond to a size 0 at the Gap. At Chico's, a 0 represents sizes 2-4. A 1 is for those wavering between a 6 and an 8. You wear a size 2 at Chico's if you're a size 10 or 12 elsewhere, and sizes 14-16 are a dignified number 3 at Chico's. Now how brilliant is that? Who doesn't want to look at the label on her blouse, when she is ironing all blurry-eyed in the morning in her gym shorts and ratty T-shirt, and see a perky number like "2" on it. The psychology is brilliant.

Here's another thing that's brilliant. Remember Garanimals? I think Sears had those. They were basically a line of children's clothing that had an animal sewn in the tag so you knew that, if you had a giraffe on your pants and a giraffe on your top, you were going to match. How many people have you met who need this system?

Chico's entire store is garanimal-esque. That is to say, they have a color palette that doesn't change much from season to season. They don't have to use animals on their tags—you just rely on your own good taste. The colors will match. If you don't have any taste, you may rely on any number of honest sales people, who will tell you if something makes your ass look huge or that you should go up (or down) a size. I like things loose. But many times I tend to buy the too-big size and they talk me into being a little more clingy. And they are right. I met a salesperson in Seattle recently who is also a teacher. She works two shifts a week at Chico's to feed her habit. She told me she literally takes home no pay—it all goes to buying Chico's clothes. They aren't cheap. An average Traveler's piece will set you back about $78. They do have sales periodically when you can get stuff at 30-50 percent off. They also have an awesome website.

Chico's began as an Indian art store. Today it is a publicly traded company. Here's the "about us" from the website[1]:

> Chico's sells exclusively designed, private-label women's clothing and related accessories. The Company operates 710 women's specialty stores, including stores in 47 states, the District of Columbia, the U.S. Virgin Islands and Puerto Rico operating under the Chico's, White House\Black Market, and soma by Chico's names. The Company owns 474 Chico's front-line stores, 27 Chico's outlet stores, 181 White House\Black Market front-line stores, 5 White House\Black Market outlet stores and 10 Soma by Chico's stores; franchisees own and operate 13 Chico's stores. Established in 1983, Chico's began in a small store on Sanibel Island, Florida with Marvin and Helene Gralnick selling Mexican folk art and cotton sweaters.
>
> From our exclusive, private-label designs to our most amazing personal service, Chico's is truly a unique retail environment. When you walk into any Chico's store, you can depend upon the sales staff to coordinate, accessorize, and help you build a wardrobe to suit your needs. All our products are designed and developed by our Product Development Team in our Headquarters in Fort Myers, Florida, which enables us to provide you with new styles every week.
>
> We're moving fast, but not without you. Get yourself to Chico's!

---

1 I did not read any of the "about us" on the website until I had finished writing this chapter. Look how closely I interpreted their business. I truly am its target audience, and Chico's truly is living its brand.

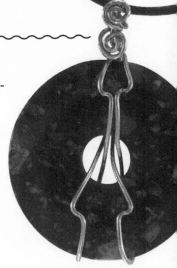

The dressing rooms are not in the back like a hall-way full of closets but rather a bunch of rooms that open into this big common area that has gigantic mirrors. The individual rooms don't have any mirrors, forcing you to pop out to look in these giant mirrors. So giant that women don't have to take turns to see themselves but end up standing side-by-side complimenting each other. Brilliant.

Chico's jewelry is all Garanimal too. If your blouse has turquoise in it—you bet the turquoise in the necklace is going to be an exact match.

Then there's the Traveler's Collection. Just like the name implies—it's a line of clothing that travels like a dream. This is where I begin to weep. An entire clothing line made of that incredible black dress fabric I bought at the Denver airport. Just when I don't think they can come up with another must-have Traveler's piece—they do. They have a mock wrap-around skirt with Western-style fringe down the front and on the bottom that I just bought. These clothes are so durable and beautiful and feminine I even wear them on the weekend.

Chico's even made the check-out process amazing. First, they have a frequent flyer program they call Passport. Once you've spent $500 at Chico's you will get 5 percent off forever. Almost covers the sales tax in most states. Plus, every month you get a catalog with a coupon for $25 off a purchase of $100 or more. You used to have to clip it and bring it in. Now they have records in their computer, and you can just have them pull up the coupons you've been issued that haven't been used. Again, brilliant.

The final touch to this incredible experience? They gently wrap your new clothes in tissue paper with the CHICO'S logo all over and tie the handle of the bag with three different colors of curly ribbon. Oh, and when you buy jewelry—they let you pick out these beautiful silk pouches to place it in.

I have never enjoyed shopping as much as I do at Chico's. Sometimes it's overwhelming because there's so much to choose from. I've been loading up lately because I know they've gone public, and now I'm worried that some idiot is going to buy the company and cheapen it. Please stay loyal to me, Mr./Ms. Chico. You have targeted me. I am loyal—you have made your competition irrelevant to me. Let's stay together.

Chicos:
Five Steps to Tattoo-worthiness

1. **The Target Audience.** *Definitely the woman traveler. Which by the way, our number is getting bigger and bigger every year.*

2. **Talking to the Target.** *I can only imagine that they did talk to us. They have a new competitor. Read on.*

3. **Knowing the Competition.** *GAP. Right. Good luck. Seeing that they left this huge marketing segment in the dust, GAP announced the opening of a concept store in 2005. Forth & Towne. Here's what the Chicagoist™ says about this wannabe. "GAP purposefully misspelled both Fourth and Town in the new store's name... and .... they decided to use an ampersand instead of spelling out because Forth And Town hit a little too close to describing their target market." Ouch.*

4. **Making Them Irrelevant.** *As of this writing, Chico's has no real competition. They design their own clothes rather than relying on buyers of the latest trends. They keep a close eye on what is in fashion and then adapt it to us. Not fat people, GAP. Real people.*

5. **Staying Loyal to Their Brand.** *The stock is up. New Chico's stores are popping up everywhere. I'm not worried. But just in case, I'm loading up.*

Chico's is tattooed on my brain.

8 Texas

Yeah, the Whole Freakin' State

Every time I travel to the Midwest (which pretty much encompasses everything east of Colorado in my opinion) I'm bound to experience significant humidity. That's when I miss Texas. Sure, Portland, Oregon (my home town) has measurable humidity—but that's from the inordinate amount of rain. I'm talking the kind of humidity that takes your breath away. The kind you can swing your arms and feel—as if you're cutting through softened butter. That's Texas humidity.

I moved to Texas when I started my own business. Why? Because I could (I was newly divorced and free of all ties) and because it was, in my opinion, in the middle of the United States. Well, actually the middle looks like northern Kansas but Texas sounded more exciting. Plus, I was going to do a ton of air travel and Texas has tons of huge airports.

Why Dallas? Because as a teenager during the eighties I was a total addict of the Ewings. I loved South Fork Ranch and the clothes and cars and all that went with the culture of Dallas. I had honestly never been to Dallas, but through the miracle of technology I found my apartment on the Internet and rented space on a freight truck for my stuff and car. I flew in to meet my stuff and my new landlord. It was June. It was 96 degrees and the humidity was somewhere around 300 percent that day. Or so I heard. I lived on the second floor. Had a view of the pool. Which sounds so romantic but in Dallas pools are as common as Starbucks stores in Seattle. They are everywhere. I've never sweat so much in my life. I had to make a sweat band to wrap around my head to keep it out of my eyes so I could see. I drank gallons of Gatorade, never needing to pee it out. Amazing. I began to sweat bright green liquid.

I moved all of my stuff into my apartment, got my TV all hooked up, and saw a tornado watch flash on the bottom of the screen. What does that mean? It's going to be on TV? Then the rain came and the thunder and lightning—and just when I thought it couldn't get more violent—it did. I lay on my couch and watched. The power went out. Which meant the air conditioning went out. How cool. We never get this stuff back home.

The power came back on—I decided I needed a reward for the move and the storm, so I drove to the grocery store down the street to buy some ice-cold Coronas and chips and salsa. I wanted to sit out on my deck and celebrate Texas.

So I'm in the store walking around. Got the chips—shaped like the state of Texas!—and salsa, the limes—but where was the beer? Finally I track down a stock girl and say, "I give up. Where do you hide the beer?" She said, "Honey you're in a dry county—we're all Baptists, we don't carry liquor." And I replied, "Well if one were to be a Catholic and wanted to buy beer, where would one go?" Turns out I need only drive down the street a bit to a "partially wet" county where I could go to a liquor super-store and stock up.

The liquor super-store is the size of the supermarket that carries only booze. Wine, beer, hard liquor, hard-to-find liquor, you name it. You grab a grocery cart when you walk in. Even some Baptists do. So I'm told. Gotta love Texas. Everything is bigger in Texas. Serious supersize mentality.

The Texas Look

I moved there with short, straight hair, my natural nails, white-skinned, and relatively unadorned. I learned very quickly that you don't just "put-a-hat-on" Saturday morning, do your grocery shopping, and grab a coffee at Starbucks. No, in Dallas the women are gorgeous. They always look their best. The average woman in Dallas could just quickly change into an evening gown and proudly walk down the red carpet to the Oscars. That's how together they are. Down to the very last detail. They are coiffed, manicured, pedicured, colored, accessorized, exfoliated, massaged, and toned.

Before moving to Dallas, I bathed daily. And when summer came along, I'd shave my legs regularly. I clipped my fingernails and toenails when they needed it. Generally a good groomer. But Dallas grooming required a lot more. I immediately joined a health club. Not a 24-hour fitness center but the Dallas Signature Club. A beautiful facility complete with restaurant, and the coolest feature—laundry service. You just left your stinky workout clothes in your own locker and the laundry fairy would wash them, fold them, and put them back for your next workout. It was there I met Darren, my personal trainer, photographer, confidant, and friend. He was 40, tall, black, built, and a little bit of gorgeous. You know how you want to clean the house before the maid comes? I so wanted to get in shape before I let Darren see me work out—but it doesn't work that way.

During my first "work out" with Darren I started to get lightheaded. Partly nerves, partly because he was freaking hot, but mainly because you know how you always brush and floss like mad the day of your dental appointment? Well, you don't eat before you work out with your personal trainer. I didn't want to look bloated. So, blood sugar dropping, heart rate increasing, my first workout ended in the restaurant. I am truly a Dallas princess.

Dallas is the only place I know where you can buy salon-quality hair care products at the grocery store. No woman should be denied easy access to fine grooming accoutrements. And we're not just talking Paul Mitchell. I mean to say all of the big-name brands are there—I think the Suave products are stocked next to the household cleaners.

Did I mention that Texas hair is huge? I mean, defies gravity huge. After many attempts to make my own limp, short cat-hair slightly poofy, I finally asked a woman in the grocery store. Originally, I was just going to follow her around to see what she bought, but I think I was making her nervous. So, I just came clean. I had just moved from Portland, and found it next to impossible to do anything with my hair—in fact, in this humidity it looked like I never got all the conditioner rinsed out. You know the look, total flat head. Anyway, the secret is in the product—she loaded me up. I'm not kidding—we're talking six different steps. The product process.

I began to grow my hair out, and at my peak—and I say peak because it really was a proud moment for me—my hair had grown into a chin-length bob that I teased up at the crown, finished off with a snow leopard-print-fur headband, and flipped out at the bottom. It was kind of Laura Petrie on crack. But when I paired it with a black silk, flowing, crinkle skirt and my denim fringe jacket and silver jewelry, well, I was ready to go to my first ever Dallas Ladies Book Club.

The Texas Social Scene

I love to read, so naturally when a lady at the club asked if I'd like to be a part of her book club, I was all over it. I quickly learned that the book club was not really about reading the book—in fact, that was optional. It was about the opportunity to host the book club and to show off your style to the other ladies. Whoever hosted picked the next book. So, when it was your turn to host, you actually didn't get to choose the book. You would simply be reviewing at the club meeting.

When it was finally my turn to host the party, the book that the previous month's hostess chose was *The Red Tent*. I loved this book—major chick bonding. And because I love a theme—that's what brand is all about—I decided to do it up right. I knew that by far I would have the smallest home. Hell, I was the only one who lived in an apartment and not a big-ass[1] house.

---

1 "Big-ass" is a term used by even the most devout Texas Baptists. It is not a swear word but rather a universally used description of Dallas Big—"big-ass."

The Red Tent is a story loosely based on Rachel, Dinah, and some other dude in the bible. It was really about menstruation prior to civilization. Yes, in biblical times women were banished to caves to experience the miracle of the menses. Women began to cycle together because, as *The Red Tent* shows us, it was neither punishment nor humiliation but the beginning of the tradition of women's going to the restroom together. It's our place to bond. It's where all great truths are revealed. And so it began back in the days of Rachel (and that dude.)

What are the elements of brand we can weave into this party? Red Tent. Menstruation. Well, the obvious—the color red. I BBQd London broil[2], steamed red potatoes, sliced red tomatoes, served a lovely red wine. And for dessert? You guessed it, red velvet cake. Red roses on the table, red napkins, red place cards. Beautiful. And then to get things rolling, I asked each lady to tell her most tragic menstruation story. Every woman has one. The one that made us all cry—out of pure joy that our story was not as tragic—naturally won. This, essentially, was my Dallas debut—party-wise. After that I was invited to all kinds of parties.[3]

I was in Dallas a month ago—it was June. The humidity was big-fat-sweaty-guy-hug heavy. Ah, I miss it.

---

2 *I quickly learned the barbecue in Dallas is not the BBQ we did in Portland. Funny story, the first Dallas barbecue I was invited to was in the middle of July. It was 105 degrees with 300 percent humidity and I'm driving there in my little VW, with the air conditioning on turbo, wondering if I should have left off wearing underwear—just to stay cool mind you. Anyway, I arrived at the home to discover the most glorious smell ever. Coming from the oven. That's Texas barbecue cooking. Thank God! No outdoor dinner with bugs and heat and sweat. Who in the world would want to do that on such a hot day? Texans call our BBQing grilling.*

3 *In Dallas they still celebrate "coming out," a practice that puts simply "turning sixteen" to shame. It's very virginal in theory. But it's really all about the big-ass party and the big-ass dress.*

The Great State of Texas: Five Steps to Tattoo-worthiness

1. *The Target Audience.* I wear living in Texas like a badge of honor. I mean, I'm from Portland, Oregon. Could it be more different? Every once in a while some Texan would comment, "You're not from around here are you darlin?" "No" I replied sheepishly. And then with a big grin and the tip of his hat he would say, "You are now." He was right. Texas targets those who want to be a part of something. Something that is ever changing.

2. *Talking to the Target.* Texas is the only state allowed to fly their flag above the US flag. They have some of the most liberal gun laws and only recently did they not allow passengers to drink in moving cars. It's a rough and tumble state and Texans like it that way.

3. *Knowing the Competition.* Well, I guess every other sunny state in the nation.

4. *Making Them Irrelevant.* "Don't Mess with Texas" Any questions? You're either in or you're not.

5. *Staying Loyal to Their Brand.* History is a funny thing. It is only known after it happens.

As for Texas being tattoo-worthy? Upper right arm for sure. Where else in the United States can you go to the Home Depot and buy concrete stepping stones for your back yard in the shape of your state. Only in Texas, baby.

9 The Huntington Beach Hilton

his final chapter is not about a brand I'm fond of. In fact, I think the Hilton hotels have really gone down hill in the past few years. And I honestly can't support something that may buy Paris another dog accessory. But in 1998, a customer service experience changed my life. And I have to share.

This chapter is all about managing moments of truth. Ultimately your people are your brand. You can have all the clever marketing pieces in the world, but if your service sucks, so do you.

Our story begins in Oregon. The night before I was to fly to LA on the ass-crack of dawn flight. I had this weird rash on my elbows and my butt. I called my sister (mother of four) to seek medical advice. She lives in Arizona. Her prescription was a cool bath and some Benadryl.

I went to bed and woke up around 3am in pain. This was no normal rash. So I woke up my husband, took a shower and convinced him to take me to emergency room on the way to the airport.

The emergency room doctor only had to look at my elbows (I offered to show him tush but he declined) to know that it was some kind of allergic reaction. He gave ME a shot of adrenaline. Really really good stuff. And told me I needed to take Prednasone for several days to get whatever it was I was allergic to out of my system. The hospital pharmacy was not open yet and I was heading to the airport.

The doctor got the name of the hotel I was staying at and said he'd phone it into a pharmacy nearby. I had to start taking this drug immediately, he informed me.

So I get on a plane, strung out on adrenaline. Take a taxi to the Huntington Beach Hilton and upon my arrival the front-desk clerk hands me a package with my pills in it. Turns out the concierge went on her lunch break to a pharmacy and picked up the pills.

WOW number one.

I decide I need to get a good night's sleep before the big speaking gig so I order up room service and am sound asleep by 10:00 pm. Again I wake up around 3am because I'm in a lot of pain. I walk in the dark to the bathroom, flick the light on and eeeeeeeekkkk!!!! This rash has spread to my face and my hands. I mean there's face, and then there's more face. Truly frightening.

As I was walking back to the bed I passed out. I don't know if it was from the sheer horror of my face or the allergy. I remember laying there looking at carpet fibers thinking, "This can't be good." I called the ER doc in Oregon. I actually got him on the phone. I described my symptoms to him and he confirmed, "That can't be good."

He instructed me to take six of the Prednasone. He also advised me to get some food with it or I might have stomach problems. Let's review. It's a little after 3am, and I need to get some food. Room service is obviously not an option. And there's no way I'm going out in public.

Moment of Truth. Your product is service when you run a hotel. It's manufactured with the customer (in this case guest) present. You never get a second chance at a first impression.

I called the front desk and explained my situation. I needed a bagel or something to eat with these pills. No problem. I'll send someone right up.

WOW number two.

Now I know that company's coming. I take inventory. I'm wearing a nighty of yellow shorts and matching top. Cute. Damn. I should've shaved my legs (this is before I moved to Dallas). Oh well, I'll just grab the bagel and shut the door.

Knock. Knock. As I crack the door open I see the night watchman standing there with a tray. On the tray is a plain bagel, side of cream cheese and a glass of orange juice. Poor guy—all he sees is my HUGE reddish purple face! "Excuse me ma'am," he says, "But you don't look so good." "May I come in?"

I let him in because he genuinely seems concerned. I start explaining that I'm having some kind of allergic reaction and as I go to take my pills my hand is shaking so bad orange juice is slopping all over me and the floor. I start laughing (because I really did think it was funny) but Mr Night Watchman is on the phone dialing 9-1-1. Oh great, now company's really coming.[1]

What's with the fire trucks? I mean why do they send those guys first? Sirens were a blaring as the truck pulls up, ambulance right behind and before I know it there are two gorgeous paramedics in my room hoisting me on a gurney, looking with disdain at my hairy legs and shoving oxygen on my face.

As I'm being wheeled through the lobby the contact for the company that hired me is up and wanting to know what is going on? She's got a hotel full of conference folks (her clients) and when the paramedic tells her it's "Denise Wymore" she gasps. "Oh my god, it's a speaker!" Yeah. Like I don't feel bad enough. I pull the oxygen off my face, lift my head and yell, "I'll call you."

Off to emergency. Rolling down the hallway looking at fluorescent lights whizzing by like weird headlights on a car. Finally settle down in a cur-tained off area. Nurse is ordered to give me a shot of adrenaline. Yippy!! It's gonna be another great day I'm thinking. But as she was giving me the shot, I started to feel really weird—not a good weird either and the last thing I remember was my back arching and me slamming my head against the bed. I went into anaphylactic shock. I was told my heart stopped and at one point I was "clinically dead." Cool. I highly recommend a near death experience.

Emergency nurses and doctors are a funny people. They talk as if you

---

1 *I am embarrassed to admit this, but I did excuse myself to the restroom, grab a razor and attempt a quick dry shave. Too late—I was shaking too badly.*

are not in the room. I'm laying there kind of taking it all in and they are running around me and saying things like, "She's here alone." "Poor thing is on a business trip." and my favorite. "I don't know if there's any brain damage, she hasn't spoken yet."

When I told my friends this they all laughed. But how could they know for sure? Ha Ha.

They explain that they cannot release me unless I am with someone. They would like to keep me overnight for observation but there is no room at the inn. The hospital is full and I'd have to stay in emergency. I have to make a choice. And some phone calls.

I'm laying there trying to figure out what to do when the nurse comes in with a phone. She explains that I have a call. No one knows I'm here except the folks at the Hilton. That's who it is. It's the manager from the Hilton. She's just come to work and heard about my morning and wanted to know if there was anything she could do for me.

WOW number three.

I won't bore you with the details but let's just say that my sister from Arizona flew in, they drove her to the hospital with some clothes for me to change into. When we got back to my room, there were flowers and a big fruit basket with a card from the Hilton, "We're so glad you're still with us."

WOWs number four, five, and six.

The next morning I got up early and padded down to the lobby to find the night watchman. I gave him a big hug. I thanked him for saving my life. I sent a nice thank you to the manager of the hotel too. She informed me that the night watchman had been acknowledged by corporate for his actions.

I'm so thankful to have this story to tell. Talk about managing moments of truth. The entire team at the Huntington Beach Hilton worked together to save my life. The concierge picking up my prescription on her lunch hour. The front desk saying "yes" to my special request at 3am and sending the night watchman up with the bagel. Of course his calling 9-1-1 and the hotel manager checking in on me at the hospital. And if saving my life weren't enough. Then they over-deliver with flowers, fruit, and a thank you card.

Sadly I've never received even decent service at any other Hilton. Which will be the subject of my next book. The Huntington Beach Hilton happens to employ people whose "momma raised them right". They succeed in spite of the organization. It's not the culture of Hilton to save lives. It's their job to take reservations, clean rooms, follow rules.

Corporations don't have values. People do. Building a culture of caring is about bringing people together that share the same values. And practicing it like a religion.

The Huntington Beach Hilton: Five Steps to Tattoo-worthiness

Yeah, they saved my life. I'm gonna let this one go.

Acknowledgments

What an opportunity to thank people—unlike being live at an award show, digging in your pocket for a few scribbles on a cocktail napkin, only to have the orchestra start up to cue the commercial before you've had time to thank the really important people. God, I hate when that happens.

With a book, you get to take your time. These are the people who really kicked my butt along the way, and encouraged me when I needed it and when I didn't want it. Thank you.

- To Mr. Beazely, who made me feel like what I did mattered. Even if it was serving fish 'n' chips in a wench costume.

- To Tom Sargent, my first and last boss. You made me believe in making mistakes. Because you're right—people who don't make them aren't doing anything worthwhile.

- To my mentor, Sarah Canepa Bang. "Act like the expert and you will become one." I hope I have.

- To Katie Jervis for convincing me that I could take a good picture.

- To Cary Ferrin for multitasking as hairdresser, confidant, ego-booster.

- To my dear friends who relentlessly bugged me to write a book: Carlyn Roy, Skott Pope, Dr. Lynda Falkenstein, and Shawna Schuh. Here's my first one.

- To Gina Nass and her sweet husband, Dan, for letting me use her talents and his arm.

- To Shahn Anderson and Electric Dragonland Tattoo Studio of Hopkins, MN for his generous offer of studio and self for the cover shot.

- To Starbucks for giving me a sanctuary in which to write when I needed to get out of the house.

- To my little dog Mavis for always being by my side—snoring. Keeping me humble.

And to my love, Mark. Thank you for letting me...

About the Author

Denise was born the middle of five children to a typical Catholic family. She graduated from an all-girls Catholic school in the days of plaid skirts, peter pan collars, and knee highs. Her first paid job was as a serving wench for 'Enry Beazely's Fish n Chips in Portland, Oregon. That's where she learned about customer service, brand, and malt vinegar. It was natural, then, to take those skills to the exciting world of financial institutions. After 20 years of that, she decided it was time to take her show on the road: to share her passion for service, her love of work that matters, and to help companies live their brands.

Denise is a speaker, author, consultant and muse. She has spoken in all but two of the United States, and for international audiences in Canada, Australia, and Eastern Europe.

Denise lives in Seattle with Mark, her love, and their "kids"
Puss Kitty and Mavis.

Design & Illustration

Gina Nass is a graphic designer, art director, illustrator, copy writer, editor and artist. After graduating from Saint Olaf College in 1997, Gina moved about the country from Minneapolis to Kansas City to Austin, TX where she worked in advertising, publishing, and marketing. Since their introduction in 2001, she has come to worship the ground upon which Denise Wymore walks.

Gina currently lives in St. Paul, MN with her composer husband, Daniel (pictured on the cover—recipient of the tattoo). Gina's illustrations can be found on the following pages of this book: 19, 33, 35, 45, 55, 69, 75, 85, 95, and 103. For more examples of Gina's work, or to contact her, please visit www.ginanass.com.

Sample

Not For Resale